CHAMPIONSHIP WRESTLING

Coaching to Win

Ray F. Carson

South Brunswick and New York: A. S. Barnes and Company
London: Thomas Yoseloff Ltd

A. S. Barnes and Co., Inc.
Cranbury, New Jersey 08512

Thomas Yoseloff Ltd
108 New Bond Street
London W1Y OQX, England

GV
195
C33

Library of Congress Cataloging in Publication Data

Carson, Ray F.   1939–
    Championship wrestling.

    Bibliography: p.
    1. Wrestling.   I. Title.
GV1195.C33   796.8'12   73-103
ISBN 0-498-01335-9

PRINTED IN THE UNITED STATES OF AMERICA

This book is respectfully dedicated to Buel "Pat" Patterson, a close friend and a great coach. From all outward physical appearances there is little to distinguish Pat from dozens of other wrestling coaches. He's modest, and has a quiet manner and a healthy sense of humor. But underneath he's more than these things.

Pat is an exacting student of the sport of wrestling and a staunch believer in coaching according to fundamental principles. He has never been content with superficial knowledge.

Pat has one of the finest coaching minds in collegiate wrestling. He not only understands the basic principles of wrestling, but he also applies them in the form of one of the most remarkably practical and incredibly effective systems of wrestling ever devised.

Contents

Foreword

Wrestling is like life. In life one must learn to adjust to a myriad of situations. So it is in wrestling. A wrestler must adjust to a variety of situations on the mat. In wrestling, however, the adjustments must be conditioned reflexes, almost instinctive responses, instead of carefully thought out responses to serious living situations.

A wrestler who stops to ponder a situation is too slow. His opponent will take advantage of his slowness. In order to achieve a conditioned reflex, he must practice a maneuver until it becomes automatic. Only unremitting practice produces a wrestler who can cope with every situation, just as only confrontation of life's predicaments produces a vital personality.

Pat Patterson

Preface

Most wrestling books are little more than albums of randomly selected holds and techniques. This one is different. It presents superior holds organized into a system of wrestling that aspires to the intellectual, rationale basis of the sport.

This system, originally conceived by Art Griffith, renowned Oklahoma high school mentor and famed coaching giant at Oklahoma A & M (now Oklahoma State) was later adopted and expanded upon by one of his students, Buel R. Patterson. Wherever the system has been employed it has been tremendously successful.

Many have tried to copy it, but none have truly succeeded. Now, it is outlined here in incredible detail. Every fundamental ingredient of its power-packed formula for success is microscopically examined. Everything needed to put any program into high gear and launch athletes on to national prominence is provided. All the sound, winning, time-tested wrestling knowledge that comprises it is revealed. All the subtleties, polish, and finesse that make the system so remarkably practical are pinpointed. Each of the innovative, imaginative, thought provoking concepts upon which it is founded are presented in clear, concise, painstaking thoroughness. Nothing is left to the reader's imagination.

The system provides a challenging and totally unique dimension in wrestling. It revolutionizes the formerly confined boundaries of this ancient sport.

No matter how familiar a coach might be with this complex and fascinating sport, the Patterson System will present him with previously unrecognized facets. Even the most advanced coaching minds will find its theories new and exciting.

At a time when the caliber of wrestling is advancing at such a rapid pace it is imperative for a coach to have an edge on his professional peers. This system guarantees that edge. With it devastating control can be exercised over even the most difficult opponents.

Adoption of this system can mean the difference between a mediocre and a championship season, both on the squad and on an individual level. Adoption assures success.

Acknowledgments

The author is indebted to Buel R. Patterson for his generous assistance in reviewing and appraising the contents of this book, and for the hundreds of photographs used in it. His expert advice and helpful criticisms were invaluable in its preparation.

Gratitude is also extended to Mr. Herman L. Masin, editor of *Scholastic Coach*, for his permission to reprint selected material.

Photographs contained in the book were processed by Mr. Wade de Woody under the supervision of Mr. William C. Dendle, head of the Photography Department at San Diego City College, San Diego, California.

Buel R. "Pat" Patterson

Introduction

Buel Rorex Patterson was born on May 15, 1904, in a log cabin in Maynard, Arkansas. Most of his early life was, however, spent growing up in Bradley, Oklahoma. This is where his interest in athletics began. While attending Bradley High School he played basketball and baseball but never wrestled before going on to Oklahoma A & M.

At Oklahoma A & M Pat wrestled for the noted 1925, 1926, and 1927 Aggie teams. These teams won twenty straight dual meets and in lieu of winning N.C.A.A. titles, which were not contested in those days, captured the National A.A.U. crown.

As a sophomore Pat won the National A.A.U. title at 126 pounds. Then, two years later, as a senior, he was undefeated and captain of the Aggie team. A severe case of the mumps, however, kept him from competing in the nationals.

Pat is considered to be among the best wrestlers ever to represent Oklahoma. His coach, the late Ed Gallagher, praised Pat as being one of the most resourceful wrestlers he ever coached.

In 1927, Pat entered coaching when he accepted the position of head wrestling mentor at Kansas State.

The growth and success of wrestling at Kansas was directly attributed to Pat. He brought Kansas State to national prominence in 1931 by capturing the coveted Big Six title and producing William Doyle, a three-time 145-pound N.C.A.A. champion. A year later he produced National A.A.U. 135-pound champion Joe Fickel. During the years spent at Kansas Pat led State to the Big Six Conference championships in 1931, 1939, and 1940. His teams placed third or better every year except three.

Pat's career was temporarily interrupted for service in the army from 1942 to 1946. During this time he attained the rank of captain and worked closely with the armed forces wrestling program as part of the E.T.O. athletic staff. In 1946 his service team won the E.T.O.

championship. After four years and nine months he was honorably discharged, but continued to serve in reserve units, attaining the rank of lieutenant colonel.

In the fall of 1947 Pat came back to coaching collegiate wrestling as head mentor at the University of Nebraska. While at Nebraska he turned out national champion Newt Copple. Newt Copple later went on to become chairman of the National A.A.U. Wrestling Committee. After only two years at Nebraska Pat stunned everyone by winning the Big Seven Conference title championship.

Pat relinquished his position at Nebraska in the summer of 1950 in order to take over the reins as head coach at the University of Illinois. By 1952 he had led Illinois to the Big Ten championship.

Among the outstanding wrestlers produced by Pat while at Illinois are N.C.A.A. champions Larry TenPas, the 157 pound titlist in 1956, and Bob Norman, heavyweight champion in 1957 and 1958. In 1965 he coached the National A.A.U. and Pan American champion Pat Kelly. Finally, he produced Werner Holzer, a two-time Big Ten

The University of Illinois 1956 Big Ten Wrestling Team
Bottom Row (L to R) **Coach B. R. "Pat" Patterson, Dave Moore, Dave Fricker, Harold Brownstein, Norb Sargent, Bill Muther, Don Pierre**
Top Row (L to R) **Captain Larry TenPas, Bob Alexander, Butch Robinson, Steve Szabo, Bill Gabbard, Manager Dick Evans**

The 1952 U. S. Olympic Wrestling Team Place Winners
L to R **Coach Raymond Swartz, William Smith, Henry Wittenberg, Jesiah Henson, Thomas Evans, Manager B. R. Patterson**

champion, member of the 1968 U.S. Olympic team, president of Major Daley's Youth Foundation wrestling club, and the first vice-president of the United States Wrestling Federation.

During his forty some coaching years, Pat has distinguished himself as a truly great leader in the wrestling world. He is one of this nation's pioneers in collegiate wrestling. He was first in 1937 to film the Collegiate Athletic Association National Wrestling Championships at Indiana State. He was one of the first to sponsor wrestling clinics. In addition to this he has hosted numerous local and state tournaments and helped direct several summer wrestling camp programs. He has been a catalyst in the growth of amateur wrestling in the United States.

In addition to all his other accomplishments, Pat is past president of the Wrestling Coaches Association, chairman of the 1946 and 1947 N.C.A.A. Rules Committee, chairman of the 1948 and 1952 Olympic Wrestling Committee, manager of the 1952 United States Olympic Wrestling team, delegate to the 1963 world wrestling tournament, and coach emeritus to the 1968 Olympics in Mexico. He has served a number of years as editor of the N.C.A.A. Wrestling Guide.

He has been elected a member of Amateur Wrestling's Hall of Fame.

Pat has always been willing to share his ideas with anyone interested and open minded enough to listen. Unlike many coaches who selfishly keep their methods of success secret for fear of reducing their chances of winning, Pat has always put the promotion of wrestling above personal gain. His ideas on how to be a winner have repeatedly been made available to the vast numbers of coaches and athletes attending the clinics he sponsored.

Pat not only rates as a great coach, but also as a fluent spokesman on amateur wrestling. He has been invited to speak to groups of coaches and athletes around the world including Canada and Japan as well as the United States.

Only recently has Pat retired as assistant professor of physical education at the University of Illinois. Presently he lives with his wife, Merle, in Bradley, Oklahoma. They have one child, a daughter, Maureen.

In addition to maintaining an active interest in fishing, hunting, fly-tying, and photography, Pat always finds time to keep abreast of what is happening in the world of amateur wrestling.

This book is a memorable tribute to him and the teams he headed to the top of the ladder. All the athletes appearing in it are former wrestlers coached by Pat Patterson.

Championship Wrestling

1
Theory of Control

A SYSTEMATIC PHILOSOPHY OF WRESTLING

The constant pressure of having to make sound decisions regarding a wide variety of problems is one of the trials of the coaching profession. The complexity of circumstances surrounding any given situation makes the selection of discriminating decisions difficult. It is oftentimes impossible to recognize reasonable alternatives or to totally understand the implications of the ones that are considered.

Decisions made on the basis of hunches, traditional practices, or prejudices often result in misguided action. Reliance upon unfounded biased beliefs, supported by dogmatic authoritative opinion or emotional rhetoric, will not assist in arriving at competent decisions.

It is important, therefore, that a coach possess a practical working basis for his actions. Then, when he does, it is more likely to contribute positively to the realization of his goals. The most practical and efficient basis for decision making is his personal coaching philosophy. It provides direction in his decision making. Within it lies the ultimate solutions to the multitudinous problems posed by his profession.

Every coach has some sort of philosophy regardless of how vague it may be. It is a reflection of his particular pattern of thinking. It shapes and pervades his actions. However, when decisions are made without his questioning the reasons why he is making them, he is likely to be unaware of the existence of that philosophy or its function.

PRINCIPLES OF A CHAMPIONSHIP WRESTLING PROGRAM

All coaching philosophies are comprised of a selected set of fundamental truths known as principles. A principle can be described as:

> . . . a guide to forming judgment and determining a course of action. It is a fundamental belief based on both fact and theory. Some of the chief characteristics of a principle are that it should (1) imply action or direct action rather than cite techniques of effecting it, (2) be a belief or conclusion based on the best facts or near facts, or on the best judgments presently available and to which men of good reason should agree, (3) be applicable, attainable, and interpreted similarly by men of good reason.*

Principles represent existing relationships between facts and judgments as derived from these relationships. They serve as guidelines for taking deliberate and purposeful action. They direct coaching efforts and thereby are largely responsible for determining the effectiveness of the wrestling program.

Principles dictate coaching practices. When projected into a theoretical framework, they provide the directing force for stabilizing coaching efforts. Consistency in all aspects of coaching practices is thereby assured.

The sport of wrestling embraces many such principles. The Patterson System is basically the complimentary implementation of a specific set of these principles. Identification of them brings into focus the unique aspects of the system. To best understand the system it is, therefore, necessary to know the principles upon which it is founded. A critical examination of these principles provides a logical point of departure for gaining this knowledge.

THE ENDURANCE PRINCIPLE. *The intelligent expenditure of energy is directly related to efficient bodily movement.*

Endurance is the capacity to engage in prolonged activity without experiencing a state of undue exhaustion. In its broadest sense it encompasses all the factors that enable a person to sustain performance to the point where fatigue sets in, thereby lessening efficiency or limiting further effort. It is primarily dependent upon the efficiency of the cardiorespiratory systems.

The nature of endurance, particularly the physiological effect it has upon developing a more efficient functioning of the cardiovascular and respiratory systems, may be revealed by an examination of its relationship to the expenditure of energy.

---

* Dale O. Nelson, "Improve Performance by Utilizing Fundamental Principles of Movement," *Athletic Journal* (November 1958): p. 26.

Practical application of the knowledge of how endurance relates to energy expenditure is based upon an understanding of the fundamental principle of intelligent and efficient conservation of energy as evidenced through the proper employment of body movement. It is only through such understanding that the relationship between various movements of the body while wrestling and the enhancing of endurance can be identified.

The importance of learning correct movement mechanics in the acquisition and perfection of wrestling skills as it relates to the physiological benefits of increased endurance often is unrecognized. The influence that skilled movement has upon improving the capacity for continuous exertion has frequently been overlooked.

Expenditure of energy is directly related to the level of efficiency at which a skill is performed. It is the ratio of the amount of work accomplished to the amount of energy expended. The smaller the expenditure the greater the efficiency. The greater the efficiency the more likely it is that the results sought will be realized with the least expenditure of energy.

There are two ways that a skillful movement can reduce energy expenditure and thereby contribute to improved endurance. The first is by the efficient conservation of energy. To be fully appreciated, this requires further explanation and amplification. Specifically, the ability to move is fundamental to competition in all sports. But the ability to move effectively is quite different than just being able to move. This ability is developed through experience. It can be developed most readily when taught instead of learned through trial and error. When correct patterns of movement are properly taught, movement is more physiologically economical, perfectly timed and correctly adjusted to produce the desired results.

While attempting to perform a new movement many muscles are likely to contract that do more to hinder than enhance performance. By properly practicing the correct movement, useless and extravagant contractions are gradually eliminated and pattern is done with greater ease and more efficiency. The more the correct movement is practiced the better it is learned. As proficiency in executing the pattern improves, the number of unnecessary muscular contractions becomes fewer. This results in a reduction in the amount of energy required to perform the movement pattern. By eliminating unnecessary movements the level of performance can be improved and the consumption of energy decreased.

In order to conserve energy the level of performance must be high. Skillful performance results from efficient movement. It is characterized by an absence of unnecessary muscular contractions. The smaller the number of wasted contractions the greater the efficiency of movement. The more efficient the movement, the greater the amount of work that can be accomplished for the amount of energy expended. The more work that can be done the longer the performance can be continued. Thus, a harmonious cycle is established whereby endurance is prolonged to the degree the skill is perfected in performing a movement pattern. The greater the skill the less the energy expenditure resulting from the elimination of unnecessary movements. In the simplest terms it amounts to doing the most with the least effort.

The second means by which an increase in the effectiveness of movement contributes to improved endurance is through the intellectual expenditure of energy. By intelligently expending energy it is possible to exhaust an opponent sooner.

The intelligent expenditure of energy makes it possible to remain relatively unfatigued longer and to exhaust an opponent sooner. The longer and harder the opponent has to work the sooner he will tire. Thus the logical method of beating him is to wear him down so his endurance is decreased and his capacity for sustaining diminished.

THE RISK PRINCIPLE. *The relative effectiveness of any technique is largely determined on the basis of the specific body positions that must be assumed in properly executing the technique.*

The success of a wrestling team depends largely upon each coach's ability to select and teach effective techniques. Teaching those techniques which have the greatest chance of gaining points while being least likely to lose points if successfully countered is a major coaching concern. The myriad of possible techniques has made selection one of the most difficult problems confronting a coach interested in constructing a sound wrestling program.

A lack of concerned discrimination has, in many instances, resulted in poor selections. While every technique is, naturally, effective part of the time it is employed, some result in the loss of more points than are gained.

Any coach suggesting the superiority of one technique over another has little to support the claim other than personal experience. Considerable disagreement exists as to which techniques are most effective.

There is no shortage of opinions among coaches as to which are most effective. Many are fairly dogmatic about their beliefs. But not all of them can be right, nor can all techniques be superior. Since no single list can be said to be completely accurate, a sound system of superior techniques has never truly been established.

Techniques vary in their effectiveness. Those which do the most to enhance the chances of winning should be chosen.

Each technique, obviously, has a varying chance of success and failure. Of all the techniques that could be selected, each will be effective at least a percentage of the times it is employed. Some, however, can be executed successfully only against novice opponents of poor caliber. When attempted against stronger, more experienced foes they prove to be ineffective. Others are of doubtful value. Their occasional success is overshadowed by the risk taken in losing points when they are countered. The chances of losing points when attempting these techniques are high.

A certain amount of discretion must be exercised in the selection of techniques. In order to complement his efforts to win the coach has to consider not only those techniques which have the greatest chance of gaining points, but also those which are the most likely to result in no points being lost if they are successfully countered.

The winning coach rarely teaches inferior techniques. He concentrates on those moves which will work effectively against the toughest of opponents. Obviously, therefore, a certain amount of discretion is necessary in selecting techniques.

In order to make wise selection, the mechanical aspects involved in executing each technique must be carefully studied and evaluated.

The performance of any technique requires the execution of a number of specific movements. The sum of these movements, when put together, comprises the total pattern of the particular technique. In executing each individual movement the performer must place his body into various positions.

A technique is only as good as the weakest position that must be assumed by the wrestler in order to properly execute the movements that make up that technique. Techniques that require the wrestler to place himself in a precarious position are inferior and should be avoided.

The Patterson System holds that there is a valid criterion for the selection of superior techniques. This criterion is based upon the relationship of the height at which a technique is employed to the positions assumed in executing it. More specifically if any bodily movement required to properly perform a specific technique necessitates that the shoulder or scapula area of the wrestler performing the technique come into close or actual contact with the surface of the mat, then that technique is not to be selected. This criterion is to be applied in the evaluation and final selection or rejection of each and every technique.

It is essential to understand why one technique is included in the system and another rejected. Knowing what should not be taught is as basic to success as is knowing what to teach.

It is a well-established fact that the most undesirable position for a wrestler is on his back. To teach a technique that places his back to the mat is unwise. This position puts him in the greatest danger of losing points or being pinned. In contrast, most authorities agree that the safest position is standing. That places the wrestler's scapula area farthest from the mat.

This criterion is used in the selection of all techniques included in this system. If any technique, even momentarily, requires the wrestler to place his back to the mat, it is not selected. Such techniques are considered to be inferior since they do not satisfy the criterion set forth above. They are not, therefore, added to the system.

The least risky techniques are those which are performed from standing. Standing is the safest of all positions. While the wrestler is standing, the shoulders are the farthest possible from the mat. Chances are that a mistake four feet above the mat won't lose points for the wrestler, whereas a mistake four inches off the mat may cost him two to three points, or the match.

In wrestling there are no absolutes, and therefore, no single rule can be applied to suit all circumstances. However, in general, the odds favor the standing position. The safe, sane, and sensible way to win is to play the percentages and gamble only when the odds are overwhelmingly in one's favor or the situation warrants a calculated risk. It requires: 1) doing those things which enhance the chances of winning, 2) avoiding those things which jeopardize the odds, and 3) gambling only as a last resort.

The smart wrestler will play the percentages. He won't gamble unless the situation leaves him little choice. That means he won't attempt any technique down on the mat that can be done from standing, unless time is running out and he is behind in the score.

The best techniques are those which gain points most of the time and rarely lose points when countered. In short, they are the techniques that are both the most successful and the safest.

The indiscriminate selection of techniques is avoided when a system of wrestling is adopted. Once adopted the system provides a basis for recognizing relationships between the elements in each situation based upon observed and logical consistencies. The means for judging the worth of any technique is thereby provided.

Obviously, since techniques vary in effectiveness, only those which do the most to enhance the chances of winning should be chosen. A limited number of such superior techniques placed into an ordered and meaningful framework of wrestling will do the most to complement the efforts for success.

THE MOBILITY PRINCIPLE. *The mobility of the body is significantly affected by its position and altitude.*

Mobility is defined as the capacity to move. Long ago prehistoric man found that the easiest, most efficient way to move from one place to another was on foot. He found he was most mobile while on his feet. He could move faster and quicker while standing than in any other position he assumed.

In a fast-moving sport such as wrestling it is of extreme importance that the contestant be mobile. Quick automatic movements are a major factor in the successful employment of most techniques.

The wrestler who can reduce his opponent's mobility makes his own task easier, his position safer, and, therefore, his chances of winning greater.

Basically there are five other positions besides standing that a wrestler can assume in performing any technique. Each of these positions permits a varying degree of mobility. They are listed below. The list begins with the least mobile position.

1. The back
2. The stomach
3. The side
4. The buttocks
5. One or both knees

All of the five aforementioned positions impose some limitations upon mobility. Any wrestling techniques that require that one or more of these positions be assumed in order to be properly executed should be avoided. In contrast, techniques executed from the standing position extend a wrestler's capacity for speed and maneuverability far beyond what it is in any of the other five positions.

The higher the altitude, the farther the wrestler's shoulders are from the surface of the mat. The farther the shoulders are from the mat the harder it is for an opponent to gain points in securing a near fall or fall. Of all positions, standing is the one that offers the highest altitude to which a wrestler may aspire.

Techniques employed from the other five positions are learned so they can be effectively blocked or countered. They are not learned with the intention of using them in competition.

SCOPE AND NATURE OF GUIDING PRINCIPLES

Elaboration on the aforementioned principles is provided in the text as each applies to the particular phase of the system under discussion. It is important to understand that each exists as part of an integrated, harmonious, and mutually complementary whole rather than as an isolated entity. Therefore, the overlapping and merging of the basic premises of these principles is unavoidable. Consideration of each on a truly complete and separate basis is impossible.

2
Gaining Control

ORIENTATION TO TAKEDOWNS

Gaining control involves taking an opponent down to the mat and securing a position of advantage over him. Of all the facets of wrestling, it is by far the most important. A wrestler can never become a champion if he is weak on his feet.

The wrestler who excels on his feet generally wins at all levels of competition. Possessing superior ability to take an opponent down has more significance than just gaining a two-point advantage. There is a tremendous psychological impact on both wrestlers. The wrestler who successfully executes the takedown experiences an upsurge in confidence. The wrestler taken down senses a degree of uncertainty.

The Patterson System represents a takedown stand-up philosophy. According to this philosophy a wrestler, to be a consistent winner, must be proficient at takedowns and escapes. It is statistically impossible for him to lose to an opponent whom he can take down and escape from.

The system encourages aggressive, rugged, offensive wrestling characterized by plenty of action and few penalties. Although the wrestler is expected to play it smart, he is also discouraged from becoming overly cautious or stalling to protect a slight advantage in the score. He is expected to shoot for takedowns, but only at the right times. He is coached to wait until he has his opponent in a position in which he wants him before shooting. This isn't defensive wrestling; it's confident wrestling.

The Patterson style requires the wrestler to be aggressive at the right times. He is told to be selective, and attack when the proper opportunity presents itself.

The wrestler, when he goes onto the mat, should be ready to wrestle and not be afraid to shoot for takedowns. He shouldn't stall, but at the same time he should be smart enough not to go for something that really isn't there. Overaggressiveness can lessen his effectiveness.

He must make things happen. He must study his opponent and shoot at the first opportunity. He must be constantly alert for an opponent's mistake or poor position and use it to his own advantage.

NEUTRAL POSITION.

The style and poise of the wrestler in the neutral position should resemble that of a bullfighter. The bullfighter, for example, always makes the first move. By waving a cape he is instrumental in attracting the bull's attention and encouraging him to charge.

Like the bullfighter, the wrestler must take charge of the situation from the very start. He must take the initiative by being the aggressor. He must keep his opponent so busy that he provides him with no opportunity to take the offensive. He must keep him wondering what he is about to do next.

SET UPS.

Knowing how to set up an opponent is important. It takes at least two moves to get an opponent down to the mat. The first move is designed to place him in a position to be taken down. It is known as a set up.

No attempt should be made to take an opponent down until he is in position to be taken down. In other words, the wrestler should never go for something that isn't good or isn't there.

One move may not be enough to set up a good opponent. It may take three or four or even a dozen moves before he will be in a position to be taken down.

There are three broad categories of moves for setting up an opponent. The first category includes those which get an opponent to move in a predictable pattern. By knowing when and where he will be at a particular moment, his anticipated position can be taken advantage of. If, for example, he can be encouraged to move in a circular pattern, it is possible to predict precisely when his weight will be over his lead foot. A side leg dive can then be used effectively to take him down.

The second category of set ups are those which bait an opponent. Baiting is a means of enticing or luring an opponent into weakening his position. It is the most sophisticated type of set up. In most instances, a part of the body has to be exposed as an invitation for the opponent to attempt some obvious move. Thus he is drawn off-guard to an attractive opening for which a counter has been prepared. The discovery that he has been tricked is generally realized only after it is too late. An excellent example of baiting is the thumb trap takedown.

The final category of set ups includes those designed to annoy an opponent in a manner similar to that of a picador annoying a bull. By jerking or jarring an opponent he can be encouraged to move into a vulnerable position. If he becomes aggravated he is likely to do something foolish, thereby making himself vulnerable. Avoiding an opponent's efforts to tie-up closely is a prime example of this type of set up.

After an opponent has been set up, he should be taken down with the next move. This next move must be employed immediately if it is to be successful. The wrestler must also consider a variety of related alternatives to this move in the event that it should fail. He will then always have another door open so that whatever the opponent does is wrong.

APPLICATION OF THE ENDURANCE PRINCIPLE

Endurance, while in a neutral position, is enhanced by keeping the head above the opponent's. This assures freedom from heavy contact and makes it possible to place weight over the opponent. While lessening the wrestler's own burden it increases his opponent's. This helps to tire the opponent sooner.

The palms of the hands should always be downward. If turned upward they are often employed to cow-catch or underhook an opponent at the armpits. This results in having to support the opponent's weight, which can be very tiring.

Energy is effectively conserved by effortlessly countering leg dives. To properly counter a leg dive the body should be moved to one side of the opponent's charge. From here force can be exerted at an angle to parry his momentum. Less energy is required to divert momentum than is required to overpower it.

By remaining in the path of the charging opponent, a great deal of energy is expended simply to halt his charge. It is wiser to put this energy to use in gaining a position of advantage after avoiding the charge.

APPLICATION OF THE RISK PRINCIPLE

The chances of being taken down are minimized when the proper stance is assumed. The head should be held high. When the head is down, the wrestler is open to a variety of takedowns since he is unable to see his opponent as clearly. With his eyes focused on the opponent's midsection, he is less likely to be deceived by feints or fakes. The back should be slightly curved with the shoulders hunched forward. The upper torso should remain fairly erect with a slight bend at the waist. At no time, however, should the body be allowed to lean toward the opponent with the back parallel to the surface of the mat. This displaces the body's center of gravity and makes it less stable.

The arms should be bent with the elbows in close to the sides of the body. The hands should be extended slightly and kept constantly moving so as to prevent them from being controlled by the opponent.

The palms of the hands should be downward and used as a bear uses his paws. This will make it easier to avoid having a hand or arm tied up by the opponent. Palms that are turned upward are defensive. Generally, they are used to cow-catch or hook under an opponent's armpits in countering leg dives. This leaves the wrestler open to tilts and duck-unders.

The manner in which a wrestler goes into a tie-up position is crucial. Tieing up should begin by walking in rather than reaching out for the opponent. Contact should first be made by catching one or both of his hands or wrists. This provides security in knowing and in part controlling the locale of his hands.

The grip on the hands should then be loosened in order to follow the surface of one of his arms toward the nape of his neck. Contact with the arm must be maintained all the way up to the neck. Once the back of the neck is reached it should be firmly grasped.

If the above procedure is religiously adhered to it will prevent the opponent from capitalizing upon a mistake made by carelessly reaching for the back of his neck.

Attempt to keep an arm inside the opponent's. This position offers better control of his movement. It also provides more opportunities to initiate a greater variety of takedowns, especially duckunders, which require shooting under the arm.

Keep one hand firmly on his neck. Do not just let the arm hang there. A constant varying of pressure will help to upset his sense of balance. Placing the left hand on the back of his neck in tieing up

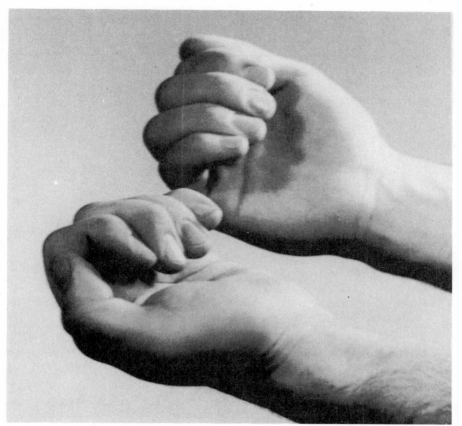

1A Turning the palms upward is defensive.

will also often have a disconcerting effect on him.

Never lean or push into an opponent. Any efforts to force him to back up, move forward, or circle should be done entirely with the strength of the arms. Additional impetus of the body's mass should be avoided. Cramming or jolting, which has no follow-through, should be used exclusively.

After tieing up, the opponent's poise should be tested. This is accomplished by moving him in wide and narrow circles, and alternating backward and forward movements. He may lose his composure and be uncertain or unable to maintain a solid base.

Any time the tie-up is not to the wrestler's liking he should back out and start again. It is better to work from an open position than it is to tie up if the opponent will not be led.

2A Leaning forward places the body in an unstable position.

Takedown options such as drags and ducks, which can be executed entirely from standing, are preferable to those which require going underneath an opponent. Leg dives, for example, are more risky than techniques executed from standing. Options executed entirely from standing are a vital part of the Patterson System. These options specifically fit into the basic philosophical concepts upon which the system is founded.

APPLICATION OF THE MOBILITY PRINCIPLE

Not all wrestling stances provide equal mobility. The one-knee stance is, for example, quite limiting. Forward and backward movement is difficult, while sideward movement is virtually impossible. Mobility is restricted almost entirely to circular rotation. While many wrestlers prefer to work from their knees, their maneuverability is definitely restricted in this position and the possibilities of attack are much more limited.

Leg dives, which require going down on one or both knees, should be avoided. While on one or both knees mobility is reduced. Rather, takedowns employed from standing that offer a variety of options should be emphasized.

In a neutral standing position mobility is greatest in a cowboy or

3A Controlling an opponent's head and arm is an effective means of setting him up.

astride stance. This stance is similar to that of a bullfighter.

The knees should be bent so as to place the body in a slight crouch. The extent of the crouch depends upon the wrestler's ability to react to leg dives. A wrestler whose reactions are slow should assume more of a crouch.

The knees are bent to facilitate quick movement in any direction. If the knees were kept straight, difficulty would be encountered in moving. They would have to be bent before movements could occur quickly. A stiff-legged wrestler does not move very fast.

The weight should be over the balls of the feet, thus allowing for greater agility. A flat-footed wrestler is slow and early to tire.

The feet should be approximately shoulders width apart. This allows for maximum balance and speed of movement. With the feet too close together, stability is very poor and the wrestler is easily pushed or pulled off balance.

4A Muscling an opponent should be avoided.

5A Having one knee on the mat places restrictions on mobility.

The feet can be too wide as well as too close together. If the feet are spread too wide, stability is increased, but mobility is reduced. In general, mobility is more desirable than stability. Being free to move instantly in any direction is invaluable.

Footwork is also very important in wrestling. Footwork most often involves shuffling. To move to the right the wrestler should step sideward with his right foot and slide or shuffle his left foot in

6A Being on both knees limits the opportunities to employ a variety of takedowns.

the same direction. The opposite would be true if he were desirous of moving to his left.

To move forward or backward the same type of shuffle is employed. After moving the lead foot forward the trailing foot follows in a gliding pattern. For backward movement the above procedure is reversed. One foot is dropped back and the trailing foot follows. Both feet should be shuffled rather than being lifted off the mat.

While moving about, the feet should never be crossed. Small, deliberate steps rather than large ones should be taken. The weight of the body should be over the balls of the feet.

Relaxation is important. A tense wrestler is slower and expends energy unnecessarily.

7A Assuming a cowboy stance offers maximum mobility.

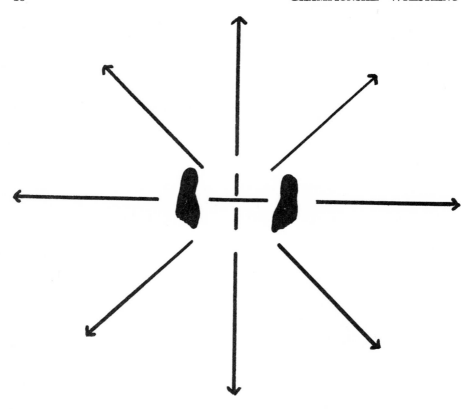

7B Optimal mobility in any direction is realized from the cowboy stance.

Ability to remain mobile is one of the most important factors in securing takedowns. Being free to move around without difficulty is essential in setting up an opponent. The opponent should be kept from moving in too close. By maintaining some distance, greater maneuverability is realized.

FUNDAMENTALS OF THE NEUTRAL POSITION

In the Patterson System there are specific fundamentals that should be adhered to in the neutral standing position.

1. Always employ the tactics of the bullfighter, not those of the bull.
2. Always use your hands as a bear uses its paws in bearing down on the opponent.
3. Always put as much weight as possible over your opponent in a tied up position.

4. Always set your opponent up before attempting to take him down.
5. Always face your opponent.
6. Always make the first move.
7. Always keep your head at least as high as your opponent's.
8. Always prepare your offense for champions. Never use moves that work only on chumps and not champs.
9. Always keep your opponent under you even when standing. You should always be looking down on him, never up at him.
10. Always have your opponent set up before going for a takedown.
11. Always avoid an opponent's leg dive in such a manner as to have an angle on him at the end of his charge.
12. Always move with your knees bent, never stiff legged.
13. Always keep your hands free.
14. Always control your opponent's hands.
15. Always walk in toward your opponent. Never reach out or push into him.
16. Always keep your feet a natural distance apart. Having them too close or spread too far hampers mobility.
17. Always back out and start again if your position or tie up does not suit you.
18. Always bend the elbows and knees for ease of movement and to reduce the chances of injury.

While on his feet in a neutral position, there are certain things a wrestler should never do.

1. Never give your opponent the tie up he favors.
2. Avoid moving in a pattern.
3. Never use the hands to hook under and lift your opponent upward as a bull would do.
4. Never gamble unless the odds are overwhelmingly in your favor.
5. Never lose altitude first on takedowns.
6. Never leave your feet in attempting takedowns.
7. Never wrestle your opponent's match.
8. Never flat back.
9. Never pull your opponent down on top of you.
10. Never set a pattern on tie ups.
11. Never go for anything that isn't there.
12. Avoid going under your opponent unless time and the score indicate this is your only chance.
13. Never lock up ear to ear or cheek to cheek except on the dance floor.

14. Never stop moving.
15. Never go under a heavier opponent.
16. Never try to muscle your opponent. There is always an easier way of outfoxing him.
17. Never cross your legs while moving.

TACTICS FROM THE NEUTRAL POSITION

Moves Used to Take Down an Opponent

FIREMAN'S CARRY

8A Drop to one knee while maintaining a tight grip on the opponent's upper arm. The head should be deep behind the opponent's tricep with one arm up between his legs at the crotch.

8B Hoist the opponent onto the shoulders by lifting with the arm that is on his spine, bulling the neck, and pulling down on his trapped arm.

8C Lower the opponent to the mat in somewhat of a somersault fashion.

8D While holding onto his arm go into a bottom arm pin. Note: This type of fireman's carry is recommended instead of the style that requires sitting down to the mat since it offers many more options, i.e., ducks and drags, when the situation changes as a result of the opponent's movements.

DUCK UNDER

9A From the tie-up position keep your head above the opponent's.

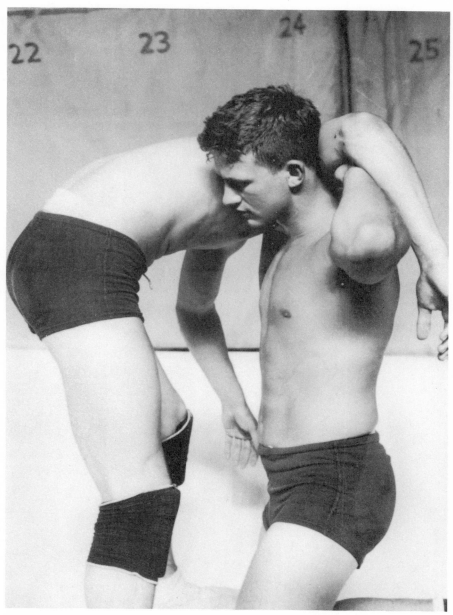

9B Pull the opponent's arm forward and over the top of your head.

9C In the same movement, drop directly forward as close as possible to the opponent's side.

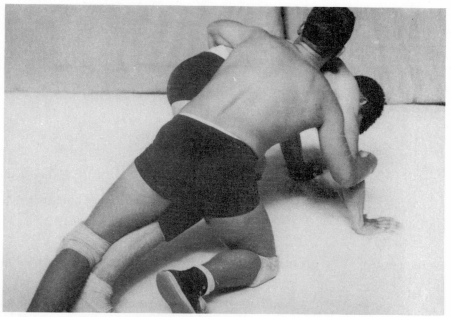

9D Continue to pull him toward the mat while pivoting on one knee
to a position of advantage.

ARM LIFT

10A Place one hand behind the **opponent's** elbow.

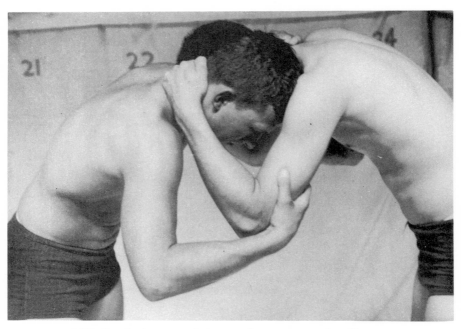

10B Push down and in on the **opponent's** elbow.

10C When the opponent reacts lift up on his arm and quickly drop in close for a single-leg pick up.

TWISTING ARM FIREMAN'S CARRY

11A In the neutral position grasp the opponent's hand with your palm down and your thumb on the outside of his wrist. Wrap your hand completely around his fingers. This makes it difficult for him to free his hand.

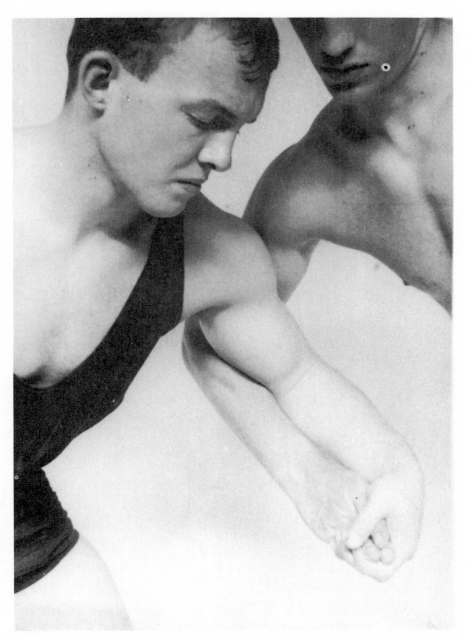

11B Flex your arm at the elbow and place it inside and alongside of the opponent's forearm. This provides you with a considerable amount of leverage in controlling his arm.

11C Drive your head forward explosively to a point underneath and beyond the opponent's armpit. At the same time step between the opponent's legs while dropping your outside knee to the mat. One arm should be jammed into the opponent's crotch until his weight is centered over the crook of your arm.

11D Keep your chest close, back straight, head high, and the front of your body against the opponent's legs. Lift the opponent off the mat and onto your shoulders. The emphasis here is on bringing the opponent's elbow and knee together.

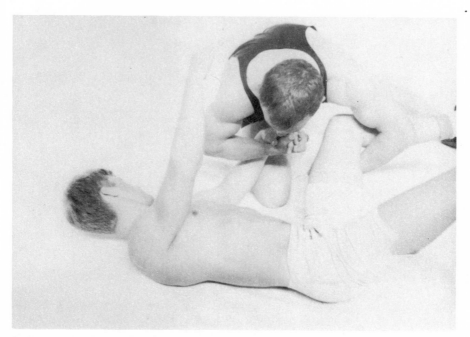

11E Lower the opponent to the mat and pull your head out from his armpit.

11F Immediately go into a pinning combination while the opponent
is in a precarious position on his back.

FICKEL'S FIREMAN'S CARRY

12A Drop down to one knee and reach inside the opponent's crotch.

12B If in the process of going for a fireman's carry your opponent tips you back momentarily, do not panic.

12C Begin pushing into him with your feet until the top of your head touches the mat.

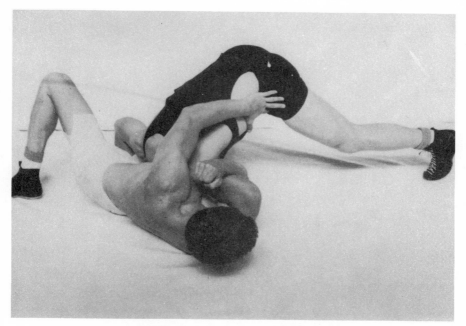

12D Execute a backward roll.

12E Pull your head out and go into a bottom arm pin.

HEAD AND THIGH

13A In the tie-up position place one hand on the opponent's neck and the other under one of his arms.

13B Pull the opponent forward with both arms while taking a long step forward. The step should be large enough to permit your head to move to a position under his armpit. Hook one hand behind his knee.

13C Pull the head back and toward him while gaining a standing posture. Pull down hard on his neck in order to bring him to the mat.

13D Continue pulling on his neck and begin lifting his leg up.

13E When the pull and lift are properly timed the opponent will fall to the mat on his back. Be alert to applying a half nelson.

Moves Used to Get Behind an Opponent

HEAD SHRUG

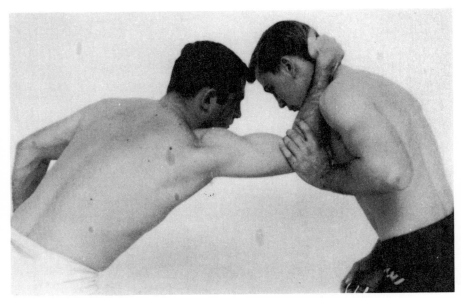

14A Secure a firm grip on the opponent's elbow.

14B Give a quick jerk on his elbow while at the same time turning your head to the side. This shucks his arm off and over your head as he is thrust past you.

14C While his head is turned to the side, step in behind him. Follow up by encircling his waist and tripping him forward.

ARM DRAG

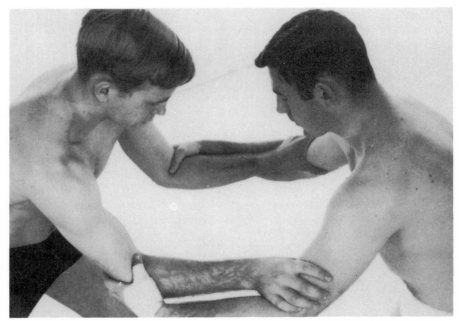

15A The arm drag is commonly employed from an inside double tie up.

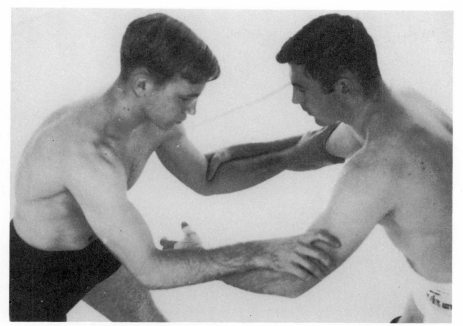

15B Be prepared as the opponent attempts to get an inside grip by releasing one hand and bringing it to the inside.

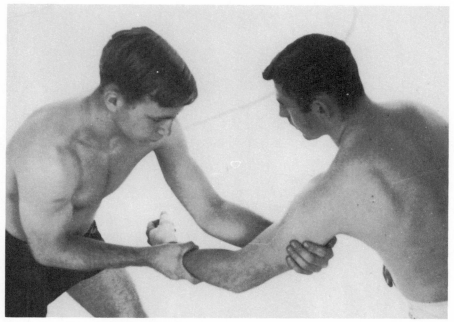

15C As the opponent extends one of his arms to the inside, slide your hand down to the elbow of his arm. Reach across with your other hand to a point just above the elbow of the same arm.

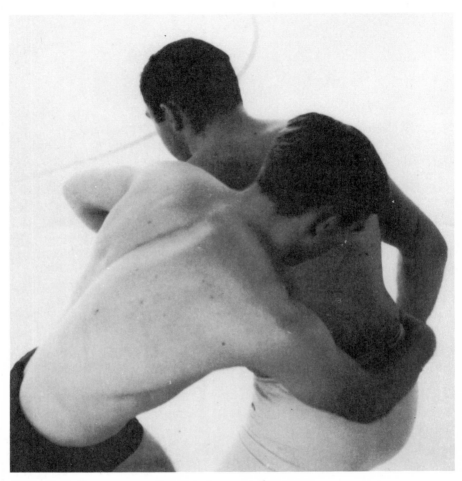

15D Pull the opponent's arm down and across.
Note: Never pull the opponent to you when using the drag. Instead,
walk in toward him. Then, by placing one leg between his legs he can
be kept from countering by running past you.

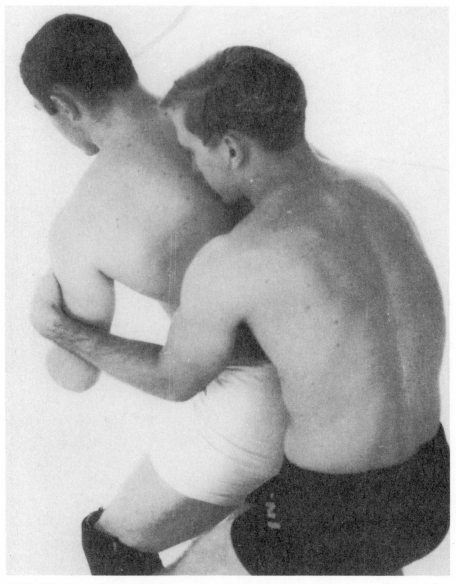

15E Without losing body contact, step behind the opponent making certain to maintain control of his arm throughout the move or at least until you get to a position behind. Keep him turning as a means of taking him to the mat.

THUMB TRAP

16A The thumb trap executed from a tie-up position. It is a baiting type of go behind.

16B While maintaining a fairly erect posture move the palm of your hand to a position under the opponent's elbow.
Note: It is important that your thumb be situated on the inside of his elbow.

16C Place your leg, as bait, slightly out in front of your body so as to appear as though it can be grabbed without much difficulty. When the opponent reaches for your leg simply lift up on his elbow.

16D Continue lifting his elbow. Lifting is relatively easy since he is already moving in that direction as he reaches.

16E Pivot to a position behind the opponent.

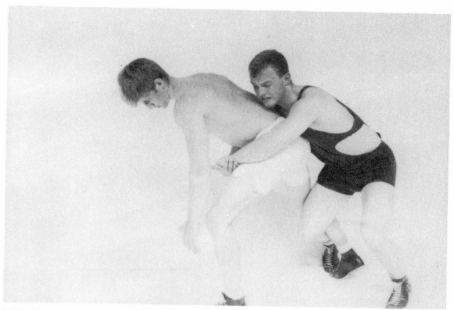

16F Interlock your hands around his waist while grapevining one of his legs.

16G Complete the maneuver by tripping him forward over his grapevined leg.

ARM DUCK

17A Lift the opponent's arm away from his body and drive your head under his arm. Simultaneously step between his legs as deeply as possible.

17B With your head in the opponent's armpit, arch the back so as to look up. This causes his arm to become a useful lever.

17C Pivot on your inside leg in order to swing to a position behind him without losing body contact.

17D Step over his leg from the outside.

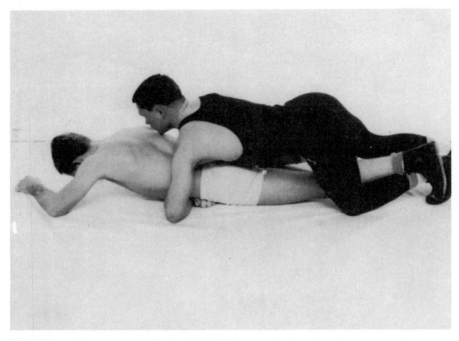

17E Drive him forward while pulling back on his grapevined leg and keeping all your weight on him.

Counters to Moves to Takedown

INSIDE DRAG

18A When the opponent happens to catch one of your legs, slide both hands in behind his upper arm.

18B Drag and step behind him.

18C Once behind him, tie up one of his arms in preparation for taking him down to the mat.

LIMP LEG

19A When the opponent catches you unprepared, give him one leg but never both. Reach across and firmly grasp his chin with one hand.

19B Place the weight of your body on the captured leg and turn the opponent's head to the outside.

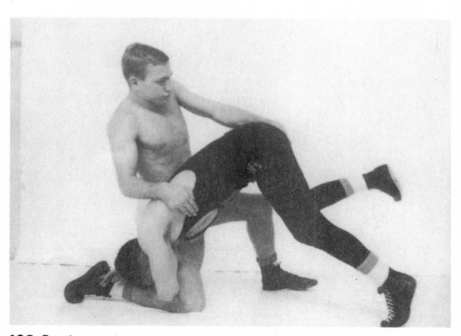

19C Bend your knee so as to go with his charge. This removes any pressure from the leg. Reach over for his crotch. Lift him so as to force him into a forward roll.

19D When your opponent is on his back, keep your head and body above him. From here it is possible to go into a pinning combination.

ANCHORED CROSS FACE

20A This move requires throwing one arm across the opponent's face and anchoring it to his upper arm. Your body should be at approximately a 30-degree angle to the opponent's with your legs apart and to the rear. You should be on your toes with your weight centered over the opponent's back.

POSTED CROSS FACE

21A Place your forearm across the side of the opponent's face and post your hand on the mat to prevent him from shifting and moving around. The posted cross face is commonly used when the opponent is under you on his hands and knees or flat on his stomach.

FALLING DRAG COUNTER

22A In the event the opponent attempts a falling drag, be prepared to apply this counter.

22B As the opponent drags you and falls back, step over to the far side of his body with your near leg. Maintain a perpendicular position upon making contact with the mat.

BULLFIGHTER

Note: An effective method of setting up the opponent for this maneuver is to make it appear as though you are vulnerable for a leg dive by doing a "jig" on your toes. The movements of the jig should be lateral, instead of up and down, so you can react quickly even though it seems as though you can't.

23A As the opponent dives, place a hand on his shoulder and neck. At the same time, move to one side so as to be at approximately a 30-degree angle to him at the end of his charge.

23B By positioning yourself to one side a mechanical advantage is gained by having reduced the amount of resistance the opponent expects to encounter. This absence of resistance plus his impetus forces him onto his hands and knees. The forearm is then used as a bumper to set up a head drag. It is difficult for the opponent while in this position to prevent you from pivoting to a position of advantage.

23C The maneuver is completed by going behind and picking up the opponent's near ankle.

DOUBLE LEG COUNTER

24A This counter is effectively used when the opponent has gotten in deep on a double leg takedown. Keep your legs spread and overhook one of his arms.

24B Instead of backing away, throw one leg behind and between his legs. Grasp his chin with your other hand and tilt him over onto his back by lifting on his overhooked arm.

HIGH KNEE

25A When the opponent attempts a leg dive move out to one side while keeping your legs back. Put your weight over his upper back, thus forcing him to bring one knee forward to drive into you. Hook one hand behind his high knee.

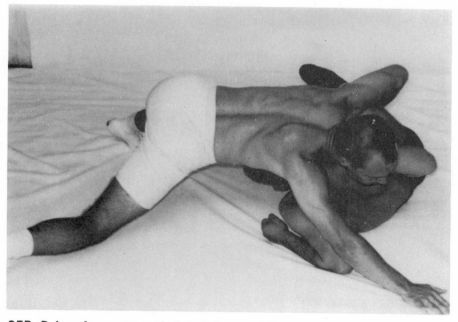

25B Drive the opponent's head down while moving further out to one side and lifting up on his knee. Continuing to lift the knee while driving into him will cause him to tip over.

25C Work to gain a perpendicular position while being alert for an opportunity to apply a pinning combination.

3
Maintaining Control

ORIENTATION TO RIDES

Maintaining control means maintaining a position of advantage. The twofold objective of maintaining control is first to prevent the opponent from escaping or reversing, and second to break him down to that mat in order to turn him over onto his back. These objectives complement each other inasmuch as the fulfillment of one assists in the realization of the other. By breaking him down to the mat his chances of getting away are reduced, while the top man's chances of gaining a fall are increased.

Emphasis in the Patterson System is upon takedowns and escapes. Riding techniques are of secondary consideration. A wrestler who can take down an opponent and escape from him should be able to beat him. In other words, an opponent doesn't have to be ridden to be beaten.

An important aspect of riding is keeping the opponent from gaining a reversal. The system encourages releasing an opponent who is difficult to control rather than trying to maintain control and risk the loss of two points and the position advantage. This philosophy does the most to complement the major objective of winning.

Knowing when to let an opponent go is basic to the system. By being adept at takedowns and counters to takedowns more points are gained in releasing an opponent and taking him back down again.

TOP POSITION.

The official rules clearly state the proper position for the wrestler on top in the referee's position. While the rules are fairly explicit, the top man is permitted some choice in the placement of his head, hands, and feet. His head, for example, while it must be placed over the mid line of his opponent's back, should be positioned so as to permit clear visibility of the referee's starting signal. Since his primary concern is to make the first move, it is important for the top man to allow himself as much maneuverability as possible from this position.

SET UPS.

Set ups from the top position generally involve tempting or enticing the opponent into making a mistake. This is known as *baiting*. A part of the body is exposed as an invitation for the bottom man to attempt an obvious offensive move. He is thus drawn off guard to an attractive opening for which a counter has been prepared.

In the riding position shown in photo 29A the leg can be used as bait to entice the bottom man into making a mistake. By bringing the leg within the opponent's reach, he can be tempted to grab for it. As he does he places himself in a very precarious position. An arm brought down over his neck can be used to force him onto his back into a cradle pin.

Instead of moving at random, the top man should plan his moves so as to keep his opponent in a weakened off-balance position. Once

26A In the top position it is important to be ready to make the first move.

he has destroyed the bottom man's posture, he should keep him busy trying to recover it.

APPLICATION OF THE ENDURANCE PRINCIPLE

In the top position there are two types of riders. One, the loose rider, checks and counters each of his opponent's moves as they arise. He has trained himself to move about on top as effortlessly as possible. He employs the easy ways to control the bottom man. This doesn't mean that he doesn't work hard when on top. It only means that his opponent is working harder.

The second type, the tight rider, keeps his opponent under tight control and allows him very little freedom of movement. This type of ride will, naturally, work part of the time, but it is not the most satisfactory means of control. Too often, the wrestler on top merely hangs on as tightly as possible to whatever is available. By riding too tightly, he soon exhausts himself.

The Patterson philosophy of riding stresses the first type of ride. The top man is encouraged to go with a man's movement and control him by keeping him off balance and without effective braces.

The top man must force his opponent to carry and fight the additional burden of his weight while he remains as relaxed as possible. He must be careful not to exert any more force than is required to remain in the position of advantage.

While on top he must attempt to keep his expenditure of energy at a minimum. Care must be exercised at all times to exert no more strength than is absolutely necessary to maintain control. Muscling an opponent is to be avoided since it requires a considerable amount of energy.

When the bottom man stands up it is advisable to bring him back down to the mat quickly and with the least expenditure of energy. There are several easy ways of accomplishing this goal. However, one of them is not to pick him up and then drop him down to the mat. Lifting him requires the expenditure of a great deal more energy than a number of easier, but equally effective methods. Also, if the bottom man should slip or be dropped too hard after being lifted, a penalty could result.

The logical method of beating an opponent is to wear him down. If he can be made to work harder trying to escape than the wrestler on top has to work to maintain control, he is more likely to lose.

The intelligent way to wear an opponent down is to make him carry as much of the top man's weight as possible. In order to keep as much weight as possible on him, the top man should never let his uniform touch the mat. His weight should be over his opponent. This is accomplished by staying off his knees while moving on his toes. This manner of locomotion also requires the least amount of effort.

The longer the bottom man has to carry the extra weight while attempting to escape, the sooner he will tire and the smaller are his chances of winning. Having to carry a portion of the top man's weight means he lightens the top man's load. He thereby unwillingly assists in keeping the top man from fatiguing as soon.

The fact that the bottom man has to expend a great deal of energy carrying his own weight plus part of the top man's weight, coupled with the fact that the top man has a lightened burden, all contribute to his defeat.

APPLICATION OF THE RISK PRINCIPLE

The art of riding requires that the opponent be broken down and constantly kept struggling to regain his base. Control is assured if he is unable to set himself. Thus by staying one move ahead of him at all times, he can be kept too busy to take the offensive.

Wrestling is a percentage game with winning as the principle goal. It is a game where in order to win the wrestler must play the percentages. Playing the percentages means taking a chance only when the odds are overwhelmingly in one's favor or the situation warrants a calculated risk. It requires doing nothing to jeopardize the chances of winning, and taking a calculated risk only as a last resort.

While in the top position control must be maintained in order to keep from losing points. In order to achieve this goal there are many riding techniques from which to choose. Some are riskier than others. Riding an opponent's leg is the least risky, safest, and most potent means of maintaining control.

There are three basic reasons why employing rides which tie up an opponent's leg are safer than those which emphasize controlling any other part of his anatomy. First, most wrestlers experience difficulty in initiating an escape or reversal without first having secured a hold on the top man's head, an arm, or a leg. By riding back on his legs he has nothing to grab.

The second reason for riding a leg is that it limits the types of escapes and reversals an opponent can initiate. He is likely to be dependent upon having his legs free before attempting to escape.

Unless he can free his legs he is forced to attempt escape and reversal techniques from an all-fours position on the mat. Techniques attempted while down on the mat have a greater chance of losing points by being countered than they would if attempted from standing. The closer the opponent is to the surface of the mat when a mistake is made the greater are the chances it will lose points for the wrestler attempting it.

The third reason for riding an opponent's legs instead of further up on his body is the security offered. While controlling an opponent's legs he is less likely to successfully gain a reversal, two points, and the position of advantage. Any time difficulty is encountered while riding an opponent's leg, the leg can be released, thus allowing the opponent to escape. The most the opponent can hope for is an escape. This philosophy complements the major objective of winning.

By riding higher on the opponent's body it is not always possible to release him. He can, for example, anchor an appendage such as an arm that is around his waist and use it to set up a reversal.

Wrestlers should be encouraged to ride in a manner that will keep them out of trouble. They should be coached to ride so that it is possible to turn loose of anything they have a hold on. They should be discouraged from favoring rides that place them in positions where they are likely to be reversed. Point wise this is foolish.

Knowing when to release an opponent is as important as knowing how to ride him. The offensive man must recognize when he is in trouble and likely to lose control. At that time he must not refuse to release the hold, otherwise he may be reversed or end up on his back. It is important that he know just when to release before chancing the loss of two or more points and the position of advantage. It is best to release the hold before further difficulty is encountered.

It is wisest to stay behind an opponent while riding him and only move up higher after he has been broken down to his stomach. Once on his stomach he is no longer a threat.

Leg wrestling is another effective method of riding an opponent. The uniqueness of leg wrestling is what makes it an effective means of controlling an opponent. A vast number of wrestlers are unaccustomed to being ridden in this manner and know very little about how to effectively cope with it. Consequently, they are less likely to successfully escape or reverse and thus their chances of winning are vastly reduced.

Yet, unless it is employed in accordance with certain basic principles, leg wrestling can be instrumental in losing more matches than are won.

A wrestler, while supported on his hands and knees, is in a strong defensive position. By removing one of his supporting points he is weakened in that direction. Then by flattening him to the mat his chances of escaping or reversing are diminished, his base is destroyed, and his position is vulnerable for the application of a leg. The first principle of successful leg wrestling is to apply the legs only after the opponent has been broken down to the mat.

The smart wrestler plays the percentages as much as possible and knows that he can get into serious trouble if he attempts to apply a leg ride while his opponent is in an all-fours position. He avoids applying his legs until after he has his opponent flat on the mat.

Granted, the legs can be applied when an opponent is on all fours. However, the risk of being countered and thus losing points is much greater. Extreme caution must be exercised if the legs are employed before the opponent is flattened.

In general, any attempt to work toward a fall once an opponent has been broken down should not be made too early in the match. The effectiveness of leg wrestling lies in the ability of the top man to wear down the opponent by having him support the burden of his weight before going for a fall.

The top man should avoid using his legs in a manner that places him in a position other than above an opponent. Any other position is more risky and thereby less desirable. Other positions may put the top man in precarious situations. They are likely to result in his losing control and the position of advantage.

The worst mistake the top man can make when using his legs is failure to remain on top of his opponent. Regardless of the type of leg wrestling employed, it is imperative that he stay above the opponent and never pull him over onto the top.

APPLICATION OF THE MOBILITY PRINCIPLE

If a wrestler can handicap or limit his opponent's mobility, his own task of maintaining control will be easier, his position safer, and his chances of winning greater.

The top man must have a plan in mind for immobilizing his opponent as quickly as possible. A mobile opponent is dangerous.

From the referee's position he can conveniently accomplish this by bumping the bottom man hard at the sound of the whistle. This bumping has the effect of anchoring the bottom man's arms to the mat just long enough to undertake a move to break him down.

Riding, basically, consists of maintaining control. Control is maintained by employing a ride that will do the most to immobilize the opponent. Riding an opponent's leg is the best method of immobilizing him. It does the most to handicap him. He can't get very far or move very fast on one leg. His decreased mobility makes it easier to control him. If the held leg is lifted, the opponent will almost assuredly be placed in an embarrassing position on his back.

The wrestler on top should be constantly alert for an opponent's mistake or poor position and use it to his advantage. He should create havoc with the opponent by constantly keeping him guessing as to what he is going to do next.

The higher up on an opponent's body a ride is employed, the easier it is for the opponent to raise to a standing position. If he gains a standing position he has two distinct advantages not possessed while down on all fours. First, his maneuverability is extended far beyond what it would be in any other position. This increased mobility makes him harder to control.

The other advantage of the standing position is that he has only his own weight to carry around. This permits him to move faster. The weight of the top man would otherwise slow him down considerably. Also, by not having the burden of this extra weight he is less likely to tire as quickly.

In the fast-moving sport of wrestling, the boy who can move the quickest has a distinct advantage. In the referee's position, the top man's uniform should not be touching the mat after the whistle blows. He should be moving first and should keep moving. While moving he must keep his legs back out of his opponent's reach.

The top man should move on his toes. He is most mobile while on his toes. He can move faster and shift or change directions quicker than in any other position. If he allows his knees to touch the mat he decreases his mobility.

FUNDAMENTALS OF THE TOP POSITION

When on top attempt to adhere to the following:
1. Always keep your opponent working harder than you are working.
2. Always keep your weight on your opponent.
3. Always move on your toes.
4. Always stay behind your opponent until he is broken down to the mat.
5. Always break your opponent down before applying a pinning combination.

Avoid making the following mistakes while in the position of advantage:

1. Avoid applying a half nelson when your opponent is on his knees.
2. Never reach for your opponent's far arm when he is on his knees.
3. Never grab onto anything you can't let go of.
4. Never move on your knees.
5. Never stop moving.
6. Never move up on your opponent's body until after he has been broken down to his stomach.

TACTICS FROM THE TOP POSITION

Moves Used to Control an Opponent

OVER AND UNDER RIDE

27A In order to go into this ride from the referee's position, the opponent's ankle must be brought back to your inside leg where it is trapped between your chest and thigh. By placing one hand over the opponent's trapped leg and then lifting up on his lower leg he can be turned onto his back. While lifting, your hand should be located above his knee, but as close to the joint as possible so as to provide maximum leverage. The opponent will react by bridging as a means of keeping his shoulders off the mat. Continuing to lift his leg while exerting pressure on his rib cage or kidney area with your forearm will force him to turn toward you. As he turns be prepared to apply a half nelson and crotch pin.

ANKLE RIDE

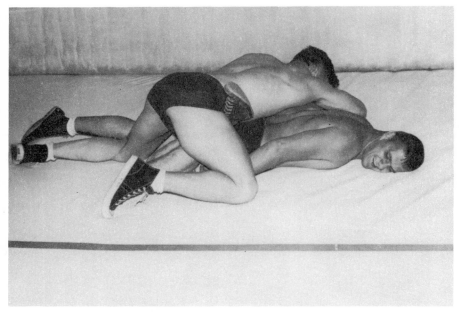

28A From the referee's position quickly move your hand from the opponent's waist to his far ankle. Simultaneously move your other arm from his elbow to a position around his waist. Go to a position behind him, pull up on his ankle, and drive him forward until he is flattened out on the mat.

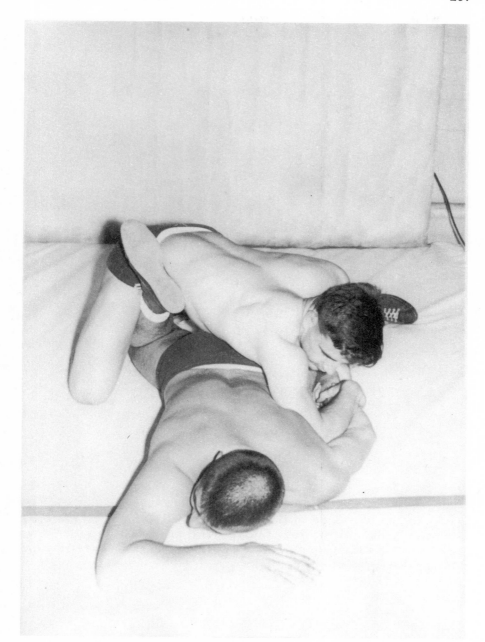

28B After he has broken down to his stomach, straddle his leg and hold it securely by exerting pressure on it with your thigh. Begin working on his upper body to turn him over.

Note: This ride eliminates the leverage the opponent would normally have for outside switches and side rolls. It also effectively counters any attempts to stand up.

LEG IN LAP RIDE

29A One of the best ways of maintaining control is to pick up the opponent's near leg. The leg is firmly secured between the crook of your arm and your body. If the opponent stands up, it is easy to bring him back to the mat by lifting the leg and tripping him forward. When any trouble is encountered in controlling him, he can be released without any danger of you being reversed.

HOOKED LEG RIDE

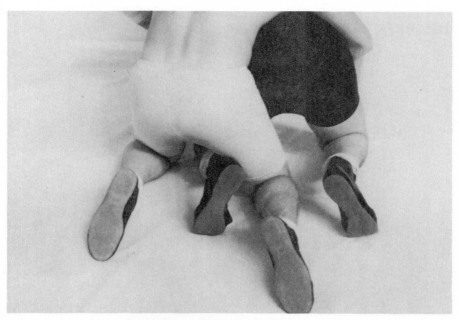

30A This is a simple method of controlling the movement of the bottom man. It is easiest to apply when he is leaning forward while in a position on his hands and knees. Begin to apply the ride by placing your inside leg between his legs.

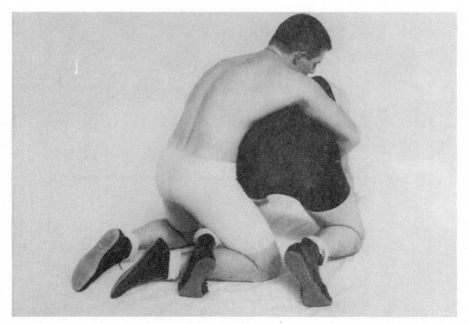

30B Move your inside leg up against his near leg and at the first opportunity slip it under. Sit back so as to wedge his leg between your thigh and calf. To exert more power move your inside foot forward.

Moves Used to Maintain Control in the Rear Standing Position

INSIDE LEG TRIP

31A Maintain a tight grip around the opponent's waist.

31B Reach down and pick up his leg at the ankle.

31C Step to a point in between and in front of one of his legs. Place
your leg on or above the opponent's knee to prevent him from countering by stepping over your tripping leg. Trip him forward by sweeping
his leg back while driving into him.

OUTSIDE LEG TRIP

32A This move is most effective when the opponent has most of his weight forward. Begin by tieing up one of his arms while placing a leg across in front of his corresponding leg from the outside.

32B Pull your tripping leg back while driving forward with your body.

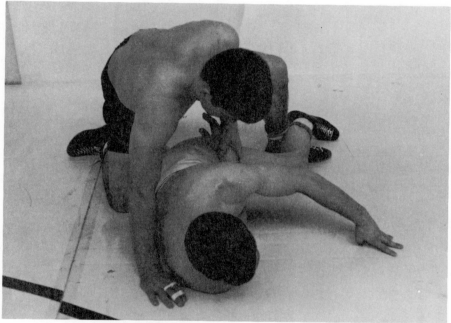

32C Quickly follow up to establish a riding position.

DOUBLE LEG TRIP

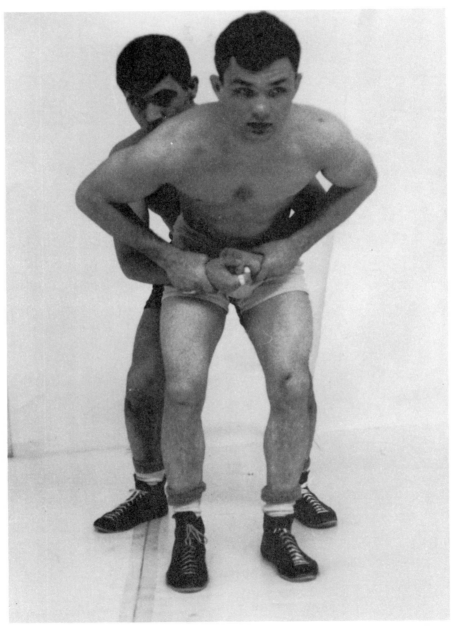

33A Maintain a tight interlocking grip around the opponent's waist.

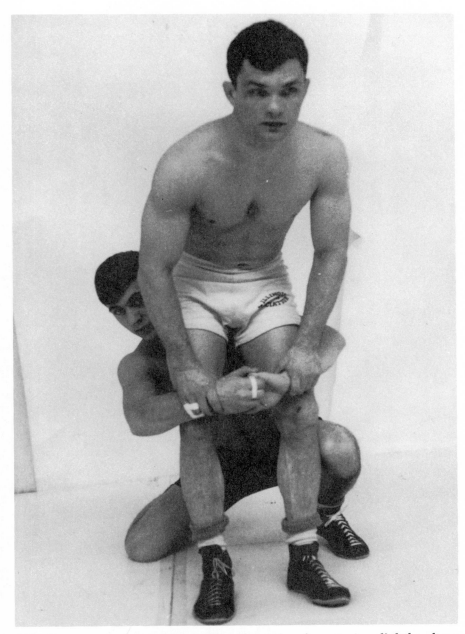

33B **Drop to the mat while sliding your hands onto or slightly above the opponent's knees. Maintain a firm grip while placing one shoulder behind the opponent's thighs.**

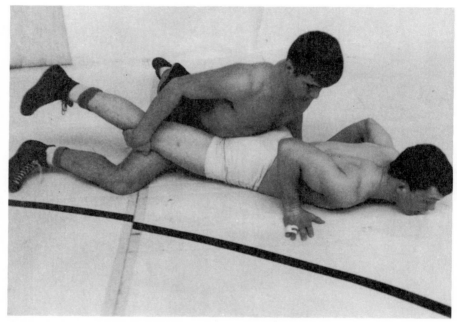

33C Lift both the opponent's legs off the mat and drive into him until he falls forward.

Counters to Moves Used to Maintain Control

CROSS BODY RIDE COUNTER

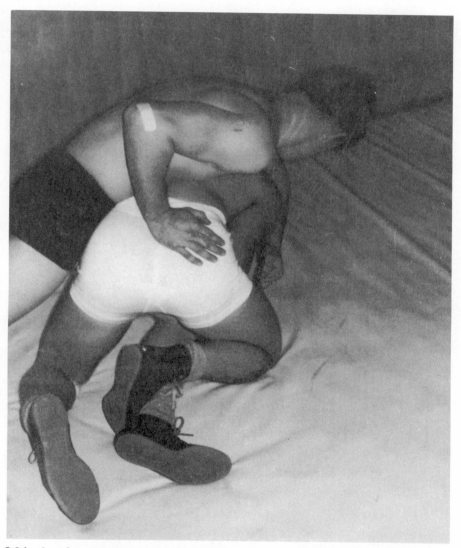

34A As the opponent inserts his leg for a cross body ride bring the instep of your outside foot over the top of his ankle. Your instep is used to hook his leg.

34B Bring the opponent's leg forward by sitting out to the front.

34C Work on lifting his leg, sliding your hips forward, and turning in toward the opponent to a controlling position.

HOOKED LEG RIDE COUNTER

35A Post the sole of your hooked leg on the mat. Bring your free leg forward and rise up while turning in toward the opponent. Simultaneously swing your near arm into him in such a manner as to force him over onto his side or back.

OVER AND UNDER RIDE COUNTER

36A Begin turning in toward the opponent.

36B Continue to turn into him while bringing your inside leg through.

36C Complete the turn by sliding your leg to the rear until both are straightened.

36D Apply an anchored cross face to gain a neutral position.

BODY LIFT COUNTER

37A A popular takedown from behind is to lift the defensive man off the mat and drop him back down. To counter the lift you should take full advantage of the forces of gravity by pulling up on the opponent's arms while dropping your weight with maximum effort. In the resulting position you cannot effectively be lifted from the mat.

SCISSORS COUNTER

38A When the opponent starts to insert his leg be prepared to straighten your inside leg.

38B Straighten your leg to the rear until the opponent's leg passes under it.

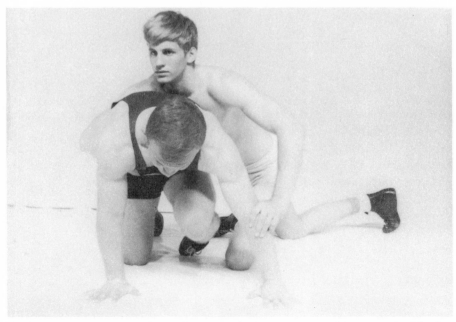

38C Bring your leg forward again and begin to initiate an inside leg stand up.

4
Terminating Control

ORIENTATION TO ESCAPES AND REVERSALS

A wrestler who cannot escape from underneath is not going to win many matches. While in the bottom position he is likely to lose by being pinned or having near fall points scored against him. As long as he remains on the bottom he is burdened with at least part of the top man's weight. It therefore behooves him to get out from under as soon as possible.

BOTTOM POSITION.

In the referee's position the bottom man should keep his head up and back slightly curved. His knees should be shoulder width. The joints should be flexed so that extension can be explosive in overcoming inertia and creating the forceful movements necessary to gain maximum momentum.

The bottom man's toes should be curled under so as to give him better spring in rising from the mat. His hands should be turned in slightly and positioned about shoulder width or possibly a little farther apart. The elbows should be bent so as to provide a coillike action in pushing off from the mat.

The weight of the bottom man should rest mostly over his haunches, not his hands. This makes it possible for him to move his hands quickly. It also discourages the opponent from reaching for his legs. His best move from this position is to get to standing while working to control the top man's hands. Being able to keep his own hands free is important if he is to exercise a restraining or directing influence over his opponent's hands.

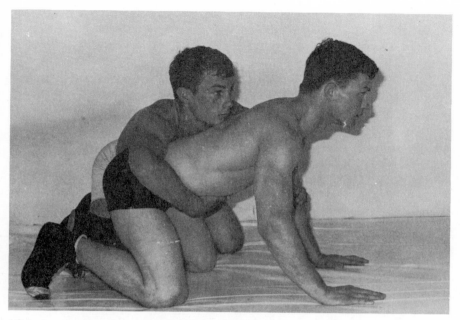

39A In the bottom position it is important to be prepared to explode into each move.

SET UPS.

The crux of the bottom man's efforts to escape should be focused upon using his opponent's attempts to control him to his own advantage. By moving a bit further than his opponent anticipates, the resulting force can be effectively employed to escape. This is an effective means of exploiting the top man's efforts to maintain control.

Using the top man's efforts to his own disadvantage is basic to setting him up for an escape or reversal. By initiating a move or series of moves that encourage the top man to react in a predicted manner, his expected reaction, if forthcoming, can be capitalized upon.

A deceptive move, when used to set the top man up, must look exactly like the start of a sound offensive maneuver. When the top man avoids the imagined danger he unknowingly assists in the application of the escape or reversal. An example of this is the standing switch illustrated on pages

APPLICATION OF THE RISK PRINCIPLE

The wrestler while in the underneath position must attempt to an escape or reverse if he is to gain points toward winning the match.

He can choose a variety of techniques to achieve his goal. All must be executed from either standing or being down on the mat. Most of those which can be executed from down on the mat can also be employed from standing.

Each option possesses a varying chance of success and a varying degree of risk. Some obviously are riskier than others. The problem of deciding which to employ in attempting to get free or gain the position of advantage can be difficult for a wrestler who is not familiar with the relative effectiveness of the techniques in his repertoire. He may pick an effective technique or he may not. If he is smart he will play the percentages so that the odds favor him. He will not gamble.

The least risky or least dangerous options are those which can be performed from a standing position since the wrestler performing them maintains a higher altitude than he would if he performed the same maneuver down on the mat.

The odds favor the wrestler working from a standing position. While points are commonly lost on a mistake made within inches of the mat, few, if any, points will be lost on any mistake several feet above the mat.

The farther the shoulders are from the mat the harder it is for an opponent to score points. The stand up is the safest escape technique that can be attempted since it places the shoulders the greatest possible distance from the mat. Standing offers a safer option than being on the mat for any escape or reversal that can be executed from either position. The wrestler who initiates moves from the standing position will be less likely to lose points.

Although a large number of popular techniques can be employed from down on the mat, none is preferable to those done from standing. Any escape or reversal technique that can be executed from either standing or being down on the mat has an equal if not better chance of not losing points for the wrestler if attempted from standing.

Odds favor the wrestler whose opponent uses escapes and reversals down on the mat. The smart wrestler goes for a sure thing. He doesn't gamble unless the situation leaves him little choice. He avoids attempting a technique from down on the mat that can be done standing, unless time is running out and he is behind in the score.

Wrestling rules are set up so that there is basically only one way a wrestler in the bottom position can lose points. Points are lost if one or both of his shoulders come into contact with or close to the surface of the mat.

The Patterson System plays the game according to the rules. It has the wrestler come up off the mat as often as possible. Standing is the safest position. As long as points are awarded in accordance with the proximity of the shoulders to the mat surface it is wisest to come up off the mat as soon and as much as possible.

In the referee's position the bottom man must have a plan of action. This plan must entail more than just one move. Alternatives from that one move must be given consideration. The wrestler's thoughts must be on an overall pattern of possibilities. He must be prepared to select from several alternative techniques in the event that his initial attempt to escape is blocked or countered.

Too often the bottom man will start one offense and when it fails he pauses momentarily before initiating another. Then when he attempts a second technique the top man is prepared to block it, and it also fails. By failing to attempt the second technique, immediately the opponent is given time to adjust, recover, and prepare to block or counter each move separately. If too large a gap of time elapses between an initial move and subsequent moves, the opponent will likely have little difficulty blocking or countering each one individually. Consequently, the effectiveness of the escape or reversal pattern is destroyed.

Seldom is success realized by attempting one isolated escape or reversal. This is particularly true as the level of ability in competition increases. Highly competitive matches, almost without exception, entail several successive techniques being countered before one is successful.

Escape and reversal techniques are valuable only when they are combined. By themselves they are, in general, of little worth. None is complete in itself, but of value primarily when integrated into a sequence. Oftentimes, when one attempted escape fails, it sets the stage for the successful execution of a second attempt.

Success is dependent upon continuity and sequence of movement. Only by merging techniques into some sort of chain or series can the most positive results be realized.

The bottom man must recognize and anticipate situations where an opponent is vulnerable. Vulnerability occurs most frequently when the top man is given very little time to adjust to changing circumstances. Time lapses for contemplating a new set of circumstances can be kept to a minimum when several moves are performed in an uninterrupted series.

APPLICATION OF THE ENDURANCE PRINCIPLE

To conserve energy intelligently the bottom man must attempt to get to his feet as soon as possible. While down on all fours, energy is being wasted carrying around the top man's weight. However, in a standing posture it is virtually impossible for the opponent to place weight over him. As a result, the opponent has to carry the bulk of his own weight. While standing, the bottom man carries only his own weight. Not only does this reduce his energy expenditure, but it makes it possible for him to employ the energy saved more advantageously.

The disadvantage of carrying an opponent's weight is the high energy cost. Excess weight causes early fatigue. The sooner fatigue sets in the less efficient will be the wrestler's efforts to escape. Carrying an opponent around on his back drains his energy and will eventually cost him points. It is therefore best to stay up off the mat.

Escapes and reversals initiated from standing are the least exhausting type. Unlike others that are employed down on the mat, they do not require the added burden and hindrance created by the opponent's weight. The less weight that has to be coped with the less difficult it is to escape. The energy saved can be employed in extending the wrestler's efforts to gain an escape or the position of advantage.

APPLICATION OF THE MOBILITY PRINCIPLE

The Patterson System stresses that in the underneath position the only wise direction to move is up. A wrestler on the bottom is least mobile while he is touching the surface of the mat with any part of the body other than the soles of his shoes. While standing he is the hardest to control because he can move away from his opponent with greater speed than in any other position.

Wrestling is one of the oldest sports in existence. Centuries ago prehistoric man discovered that the easiest, most efficient, and quickest way to move from one place to another is on the feet. There are some wrestlers who ignore this fact. They fail to either recognize the general concepts involved, or lack imagination on what to do when standing.

It behooves the bottom man to get an escape or reversal under way very quickly, before the top man initiates a move to break him down. He should not stay down in the referee's position any longer than is absolutely necessary. His best defense is to move so fast and so hard that the man on top is completely occupied with trying to maintain his position and has no time or opportunity to employ a breakdown. The bottom man is difficult to control when he is constantly moving with vigor and drive.

The wrestler who falls or who is easily forced onto his back, buttocks, side, or stomach will not be in a position to take advantage of escape and reversal possibilities.

The bottom man is most mobile in a standing position. His capacity to move fast is much greater while standing than in any other position.

The five positions to avoid act as a guide for the selection of escape and reversal techniques.

Once this list of positions to avoid has been adopted, the following procedure must be honored. If broken down to his side or stomach, the wrestler must get back to all fours, and stand up. The idea is to get on one's feet as soon as possible. In a standing position he has more mobility than he does while in any of the aforementioned five positions. He has extended his capacity for maneuverability far beyond what it would be in any of the five positions to avoid. This makes him harder to control.

The following is a list of fundamentals that should be adhered to regardless of which method of standing up is employed.

1. Always keep the head up and back straight.
2. Always use two hands to control one of the opponent's.
3. Always keep the feet moving in short choppy steps.
4. Always keep the elbows close to the sides of the body.
5. Always keep plenty of mat space ahead of you.

Some of the things that should be avoided when standing up are:

1. Never bring the hips up first.
2. Never swing the arms out away from the sides of the body.
3. Never spread the legs.
4. Never stand still.
5. Never move in a straight line.

Most escapes from down on the mat can also be used from standing. However, there is less of a risk when they are employed from standing. This plus the fact that standing up is less tiring and has fewer limitations on mobility accounts for its popularity in collegiate wrestling.

FUNDAMENTALS OF THE BOTTOM POSITION

The following is a list of fundamentals that should always be employed from the bottom position.

1. Always keep your opponent on the defensive.
2. Always keep your hands and legs free.

3. Always work from a position with your body weight over your legs, not over your hands.
4. Always come up to standing with your head up first.
5. Always keep your altitude as high as possible.
6. Always move from the referee's position as the whistle blows.
7. Always move farther than your opponent anticipates.
8. Always keep your elbows in and back straight when coming up off the mat.
9. Always move with short, choppy steps when on your feet.
10. Always move in circles when standing so as not to be forced off the mat.

While in the bottom position there are certain things that should never be done.

1. Never lie flat on your stomach.
2. Never lose altitude first.
3. Never get in a position on your back, buttocks, or side.
4. Never permit your opponent to make you carry his weight.
5. Never stay on your hands and knees any longer than necessary.
6. Never stand still when your opponent is behind you.
7. Never turn your back to the mat.
8. Never get your head lower than your hind quarters.

TACTICS FROM THE BOTTOM POSITION

Moves Used to Escape from or Reverse an Opponent

INSIDE LEG STAND UP

40A In the referee's position your weight is over your knees and not supported by your hands. This makes it possible for you to move your hands quickly. Your palms are turned in slightly and approximately shoulder's width apart. Your elbows are bent so as to provide a spring-like action in rising from the mat.

40B Straighten your back while stepping forward with your inside leg. As the top man attempts to counter by reaching over your inside arm, raise your elbow. At the same time grasp his wrist to prevent him from locking his hands.
Note: Do not permit your head to drop or get close to your inside knee. If you do you may be caught in a cradle counter.

40C Hold the opponent's arm away from your body. Bring your other hand back for maximum control in forcing the opponent's arm to a position behind your back.

40D Loosen the opponent's grip that is around your waist. Keep your feet moving in short choppy steps.

40E Turn quickly to face the opponent while maintaining control of his hand.

JUMPING JACK STAND UP

41A Proper position prior to standing up requires that your head be kept up and your back slightly curved. Your knees are shoulder's width apart. Your weight is pushed back over your haunches with your toes curled under.

41B If the top man pushes you forward use the momentum to jump to a position where your elbows are in between your legs. By having moved a bit further than the opponent anticipates an escape is facilitated.

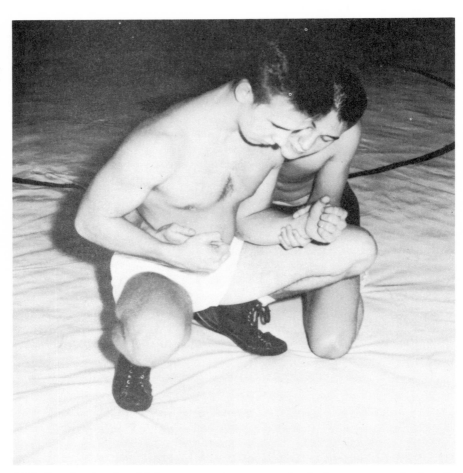

41C Emphasis should be on gaining control of the opponent's hands. Grasp the opponent's fingers that are around your waist and peel the hand off. Begin moving up to standing.

41D Upon standing, your inside arm is freed by rotating your wrist in a clockwise fashion against the opponent's thumb. Simultaneously pull the opponent's other hand away from around your waist.

Note: Your chances of escapes can now be increased if you move in a circular pattern to prevent the top man from forcing you off the edge of the mat. It is important that you do not let go of his hand until you are completely free.

BUMP BACK STAND UP

42A In the referee's position your toes are tucked under and your buttocks placed as close to your heels as possible. Your back is hunched, your neck is bulled, and your hands are placed on the mat as close to your knees as is legally possible. Only a fraction of your weight is over your hands.

42B Push back until you are balanced on your toes with your hands and arms in close to your body.

42C Your head is kept up and your back straightened to prevent the top man from applying a cradle. By thrusting your inside elbow back to the side of your body the top man is prevented from reaching under to connect his hands.

42D When coming up off the mat your shoulders are thrown back to relieve the burden of the opponent's weight. Rise quickly, keeping your spine straight. While the opponent is attempting to interlock his hands, your far arm is brought across in front of your body in order to grasp his wrist.

42E Your feet are a normal distance apart with your knees bent slightly. Your inside arm is used to grasp the opponent's hand and force it behind your back. Keep your feet moving.

Note: When the stand up is done properly the opponent is unable to successfully lock his hands around your waist. It is foolish to have to work to break an opponent's grip when initially he could be prevented from locking his hands together.

42F It is now very difficult for your opponent to prevent you from escaping since he has only one arm around your waist. Grasp the fingers of that hand and begin to remove it from your waist.

42G Turn by pivoting quickly. The opponent's hand is controlled until you are facing him.

ANKLE HIDER

43A This tactic is effective against an opponent who attempts an ankle ride.

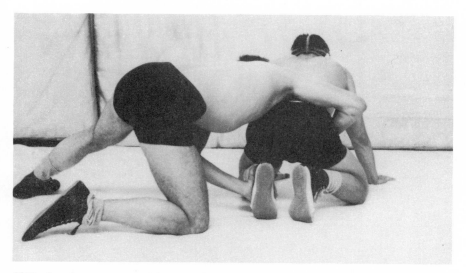

43B As the opponent lowers his head and reaches for your ankle be prepared to shift your weight to the rear.

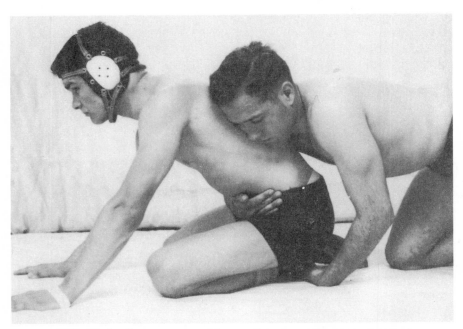

43C Sit back on your ankle until it is under your buttocks.

43D Bring your outside leg forward while sliding your ankle out to the front beyond the opponent's reach. Simultaneously move to a balanced position above your opponent. Keep your head elevated and post an arm to one side.

43E Swing one of your legs over the other in executing a swift turn
to a neutral position.

WHIZZER

44A Swing your inside arm, in a windmill motion, over the opponent's arm which is across your back. Keep your head and shoulders above your opponent's.

Note: When using the whizzer be on the offensive. To be successful you must be the aggressor. Do not, however, push into the opponent or he will roll with you. Instead, constantly lead him forward in a circular pattern.

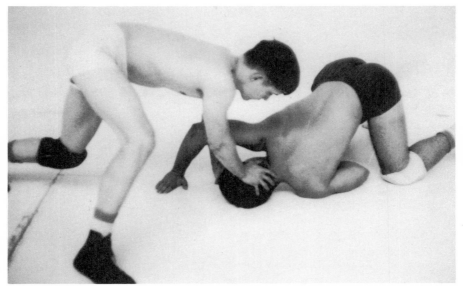

44B Push the opponent's head down with your outside arm and swing your hips out to the front until you are facing him.

POSTED SWITCH

45A This move is more effective than the regular switch since it can be effectively used by a short or tall man and has few ways of being countered.

45B Move your inside leg to a position under your hips.

45C Bring both your feet to the front while elevating your shoulders over the opponent's head and shoulders.

45D Post one hand on the mat and begin to turn to the rear.

45E Once behind the opponent pick up one of his ankles and quickly raise his leg off the mat.

Moves Used to Terminate Control in the Rear Standing Position

BACK BREAKER

46A Firmly grasp your opponent's hands when he is standing close behind you.

46B Lift his hands while simultaneously dropping your weight. This will position his arms high on your chest and allow you to move your hips freely.

46C Rotate your hips to one side while swinging one of your legs in behind your opponent's legs. This traps his leg to the front.

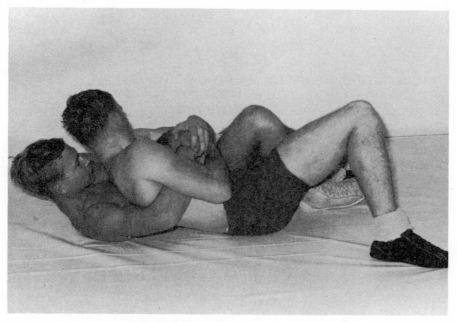

46D Swing your inside arm back while turning sharply in toward the opponent. As he is tripped continue turning to a position of advantage.

STANDING CROSS ARM ROLL

47A The opponent is set up for this move when he pushes into you. When he does, grab one of his wrists with your opposite hand.

47B Bring your other hand across and post it on the mat in front of your opposite foot. At the same time place one of your legs along the outside of the opponent's ankle.

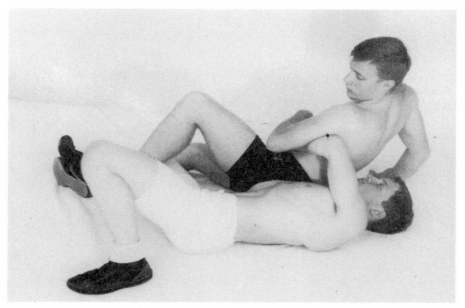

47C Roll the opponent onto the mat. Begin to shift your weight to a position of being on top while maintaining control of his hand to avoid the possibility of his escaping.

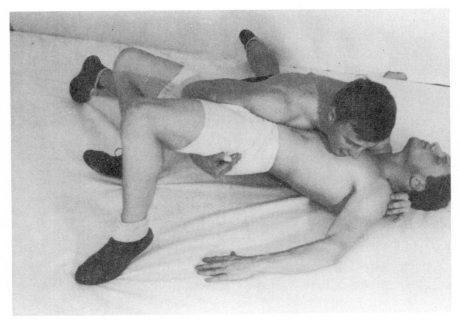

47D Continue to turn your hips while establishing a pinning combination on top.

STANDING SWITCH

Note: This move is commonly set up by faking to one side with a hip rotation and then coming back quickly to the other side to execute the switch. When the opponent avoids the imagined danger by shifting to one side he places himself in a vulnerable position for the standing switch.

48A Turn and begin to insert a hand between the opponent's legs.

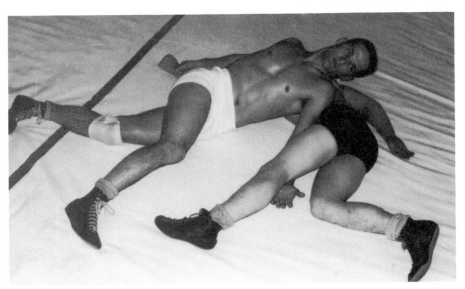

48B Upon making contact with the mat, turn without hesitation and begin working up to a position of advantage on the reversed opponent.

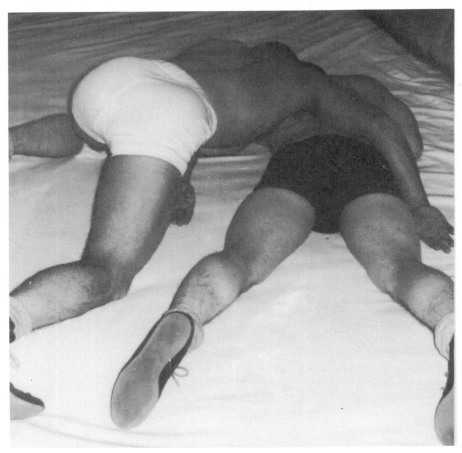

48C Drop quickly from standing to the mat. Lean back, thereby establishing a considerable amount of leverage on the opponent's shoulder.

HIPLOCK

49A Move to one side of the opponent's body.

49B Step across in front of him with your inside leg.

49C Throw him to the mat by lifting and pulling him over your inside hip.
Note: After the opponent is on the mat a pinning combination can readily be gained by securing a hold on his arms while spreading your legs wide for support.

Counters to Moves Used to Terminate Control

SWITCH COUNTER

50A This counter, commonly referred to as the limp arm, is one of the simplest to apply.

50B As the opponent starts to reach back, straighten your legs.

50C When he turns, windmill your one arm behind his head and the other to a position between his legs.

50D Immediately apply a cradle pin.

SHORT SIT OUT COUNTER

51A This counter is initiated from a position behind the sitting opponent. Press the weight of your body up against the opponent's back by
bumping into him. This will force him forward into a jackknife position, thus momentarily restricting him from turning in or out.

51B Quickly spin to the front using the opponent's back as a means
of pivoting. Reach inside his thighs to drive him over onto his back.

5
Ultimate Control

Historically, the original objective of wrestling was to pin the opponent. However, as the sport gained popularity, it soon became evident that in many instances a pin would not result. Consequently, a system of awarding points was devised for those matches where no fall occurred. Thus the concept of winning began to override the objective of pinning.

Today there are not many falls in collegiate wrestling due to the smartness and toughness of the competition. Nobody takes a good wrestler down and pins him. When a good wrestler is caught on his back it is generally because he attempts something foolish. Oftentimes a wrestler can be baited into making a mistake and end up on his back in a pinning hold. For example, while in a cross body ride the bottom man can be enticed into reaching back for the top man's head when he lowers it. His arm is then secured and he is rolled back into a guillotine.

No one denies that as long as a fall counts six points for the team as compared with three points for a decision, it will remain important. Nevertheless, in top notch competition the opportunities to turn the opponent onto his back are not very frequent. The majority of college bouts are won by decision.

Although it is desirable to pin an opponent, there is nothing sacred about a pin. The Patterson System holds winning to be primary. The pin is considered but one method of winning.

52A Applying a guillotine after having baited the opponent into reaching back.

APPLICATION OF THE ENDURANCE PRINCIPLE

A most important factor in pinning is the top man's body weight. By bearing down with as much weight as possible the top man can easily fatigue his opponent. The more weight that can be brought to bear in the application of a pinning hold, the more exhausting it is for the opponent to escape. Weight can be added to most pinning holds by lifting on the opponent's head. Lifting his head off the mat makes it difficult for him to bridge.

The more efficiently the pinning hold is applied, the more energy the opponent has to expand attempting to escape. A half nelson, for example, is most effectively applied by driving the arm around the opponent's neck as far and as deep as possible while he is lying on his side. Then as he is rolled over onto his back the pressure of the hold will increase significantly.

APPLICATION OF THE RISK PRINCIPLE

A good wrestler is never content with merely riding an opponent.

He is, instead, taking advantage of every safe opportunity to turn him over onto his back.

The ultimate in control of an opponent is the fall. While it is always best to work for a fall, it must be done in a safe, sane, and sensible way. The safe, sane, and sensible way is to first break the opponent down to his stomach before applying a pinning combination.

An opponent is least dangerous while he is flattened out on his stomach. He is more dangerous while on his hands and knees. He is the most dangerous while standing. The reason is that the higher his altitude, the farther his shoulders are from the surface of the mat. The farther his shoulders are from the mat, the harder it is to control him. The harder it is to control him, the more difficult it is to gain points against him for a near fall or to gain a fall.

APPLICATION OF THE MOBILITY PRINCIPLE

The secret to pinning success is to keep the opponent on his back. If he is kept on his back long enough he will be pinned. It is not always possible, however, to hold a man on his back with the same hold for very long. Therefore, being able to change from one pinning combination to another is essential.

If an opponent is about to escape from one pinning combination it is imperative to be able to shift quickly to another. This requires a great deal of mobility.

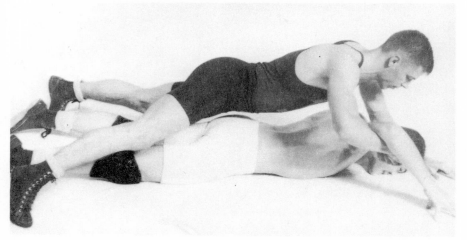

53A Applying a half nelson after having broken the opponent down to the mat.

In most situations the wrestler applying the pinning combination has the greatest mobility when his body is at a right angle to the opponent and he is moving on the toes. In this position he is less likely to be tipped or rolled over, and can operate better in terms of keeping his opponent constantly in trouble on his back.

FUNDAMENTALS OF THE PINNING POSITION

When working for a pin, the wrestler should adhere to the following:

1. Always keep your weight on the opponent when pinning him.
2. Always stay up off your knees and on your toes when pinning.
3. Always work to a perpendicular position to turn an opponent over onto his back.
4. Always sink the half nelson while the opponent is on his side prior to turning him onto his back.

To insure success in pinning, the wrestler should avoid making the following mistakes:

1. Avoid applying a half nelson when the opponent is on his knees.
2. Never stay with a pinning combination too long; be prepared to shift to another to cope with changing circumstances.
3. Avoid allowing the knees to touch the mat when applying a pinning hold.
4. Avoid being forced into a position parallel to the opponent's body while pinning him.

TACTICS FROM THE PINNING POSITION

Moves Used to Pin an Opponent

HALF NELSON
Note: In turning the opponent over from his stomach to his back it is important that your hand be on the top of his head instead of on the nape of his neck. This will provide you with greater leverage to pry him over. Then when you have his shoulders perpendicular to the mat, slip your arm in deep around the back of his neck until your elbow is directly behind his head and your hand is resting on his chest.

54A Remain perpendicular and lift on the opponent's head to keep him from bridging. Your feet should be spread with your knees off the mat. This places your weight on the opponent's chest while helping to keep you mobile. Push off your toes and maintain a right angle to the opponent regardless of how much shifting he does.

THREE-QUARTER NELSON

Note: A fatigued opponent will often lower his head or allow it to droop to the mat. This presents a good opportunity to use the three-quarter nelson. To apply the pin, your outside arm is placed under the opponent's near arm. Your other arm is moved under his chest and your hands are interlocked behind his neck. By your pulling his head down and straddling his near leg he is forced into a jackknife position on his back.

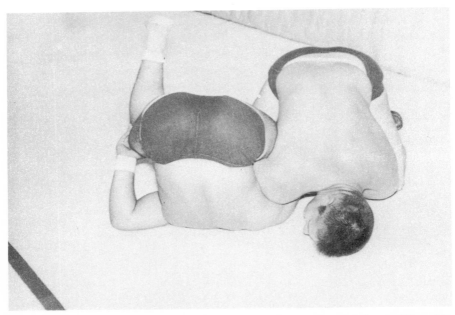

55A Keep the opponent's shoulders pinned to the mat by pulling his inside leg away from his body with your inside leg. His cheek should be up against the side of your knee.

BOTTOM ARM

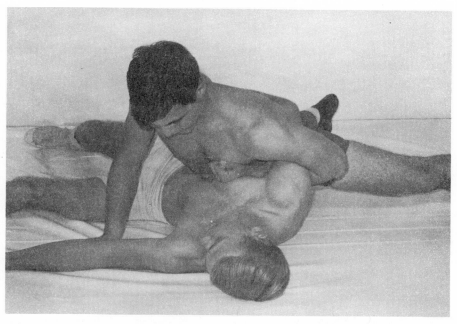

56A Grapevine the opponent's near arm and place your fist in the center of his chest. Lift on his arm to prevent him from turning into you. Use your opposite arm as a brace to keep him from pulling you off balance. Your legs are spread and your weight is over him at all times.

REVERSE HALF NELSON TO HALF NELSON

57A Keep your weight over your opponent, thus making it difficult for him to move. Stay up on your toes.

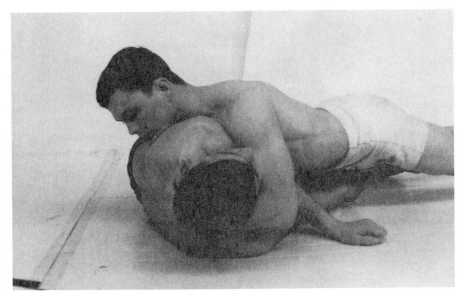

57B If he succeeds in turning into you do not insist on keeping the reverse half nelson.

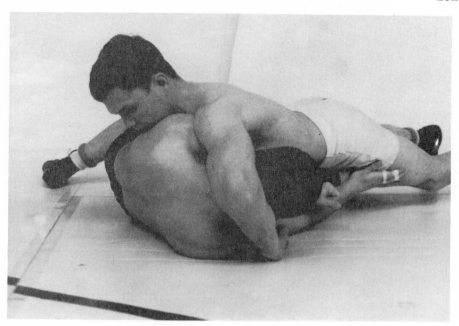

57C Shift quickly to the half nelson by bringing your arm around to the far side of his head and the back of his neck.

57D Drive forward while lifting his head up off the mat.

HALF NELSON TO BOTTOM ARM

58A If while you hold the opponent down in a half nelson pin he begins to escape by rolling in toward you, be prepared to move into another pinning hold.

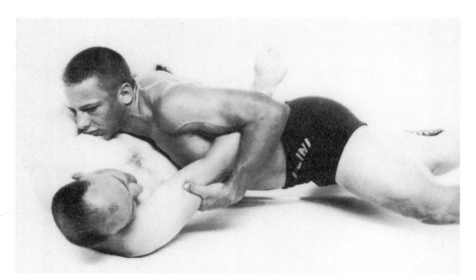

58B As he turns in, release the half nelson by moving your arm from the back of his neck to his upper arm. Trap his arm in between your elbow and the side of your body. By shifting your weight toward his head and keeping your body low, you can force his shoulders back to the mat.

LEG TURNOVER #1

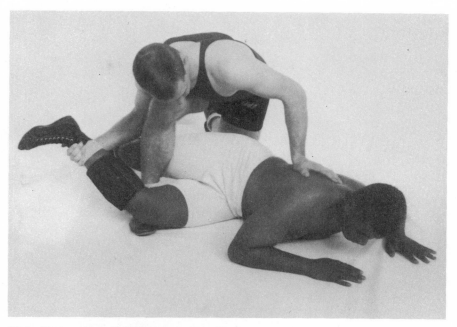

59A This move is effective against an opponent who is flattened out on the mat and will not allow you an opening to apply a pinning combination. Lift up on one of his ankles and place a foot in between his legs.

59B Continue to lift his leg using both hands.

59C As he turns onto his back apply a bottom arm pin.

LEG TURNOVER #2

60A On occasion the opponent may be lying on his stomach with his arms in tightly to his sides, thus making it very difficult to turn him over. From this position, quickly turn and face toward his legs. Sit down suddenly on the middle of his back so you are straddling his body with your legs. This move will have a tendency to startle him, thus making the turnover easier to accomplish. Care must be taken, however, not to bounce too heavily onto his back. Such a mistake could result in you being penalized for unnecessary roughness.

60B Reach down and grasp one of his legs just above the knee. Lift the leg outward first so as not to injure his spine.

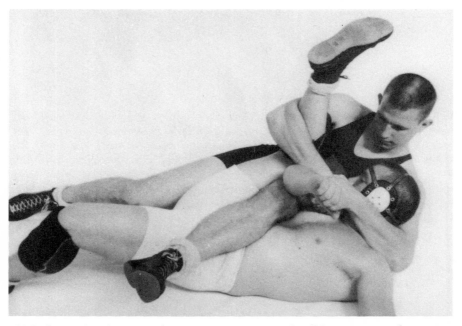

60C Bring his leg up, thus creating a considerable amount of pressure on his back. This will force him to turn toward you. As he turns, place one arm around behind his head, interlock your hands, and fall back to a cradle pin.

FIGURE FOUR HEAD SCISSORS

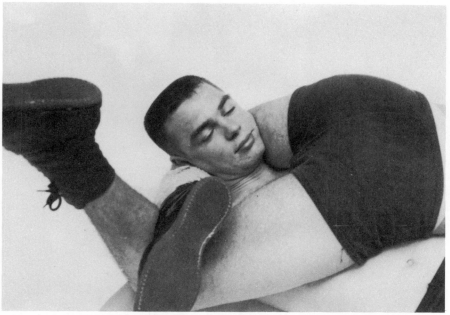

61A This pin is very effective, but difficult to secure. Once the opponent has been placed in it, it is important that his head be lifted off the mat in order to assist in holding his shoulders down.

CRADLE

62A Interlock your arms to assist in bringing the opponent's head to his knee. Use your outside leg as a brace to keep him on his back.

LEG SPLIT

63A To pin the opponent your body must be as close to the upper portion of his back as possible. By using your far arm and leg as braces, you can exert pressure forward to keep him on his shoulders.

GUILLOTINE

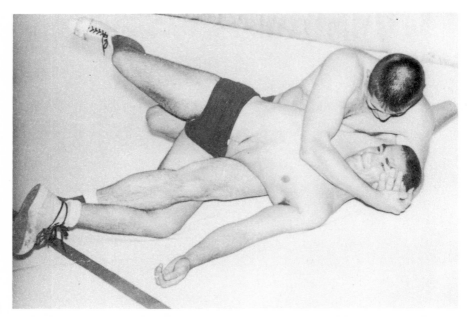

64A This pin is most effective when you wrap both your arms around the top of the opponent's head and pull him in to you while straightening the grapevined leg. Your other leg may be used as a brace to keep you above him or interlaced as a means of securing the hold more firmly.

Counters to Moves Used to Pin

GOING FROM STOMACH TO KNEES

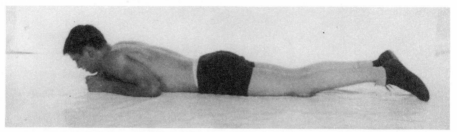

65A In order to avoid a pin it is necessary to recover from your stomach to your hands and knees. Begin by keeping your arms in close to your sides so as to keep the opponent from inserting an arm.

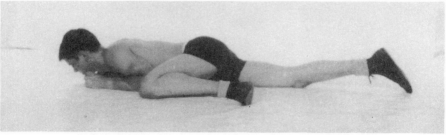

65B Bring one knee up to the corresponding elbow.

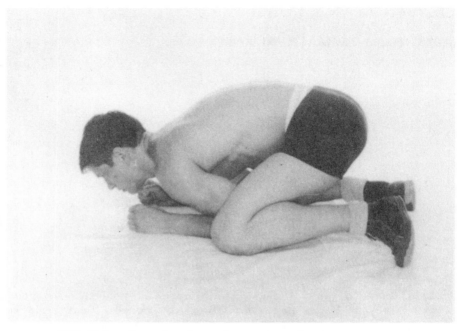

65C Bring the other knee forward in the same manner.

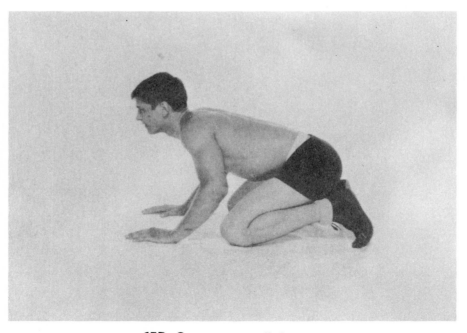

65D Come up to all fours.

GUILLOTINE COUNTER

66A When the opponent starts to reach for your far arm from a cross body ride, put weight on it. Do not allow him to lift it from the mat. At the same time hook the instep of your foot over his ankle.

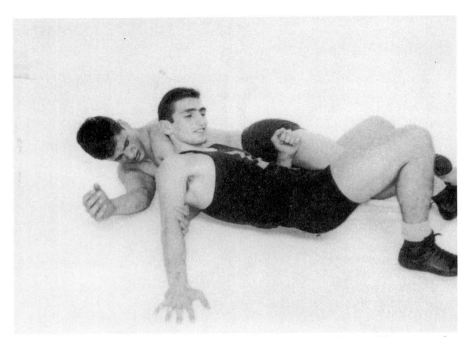

66B Drop to your side so as to place your head and shoulder over the opponent's extended arm. Drive your inside arm between his body and yours.

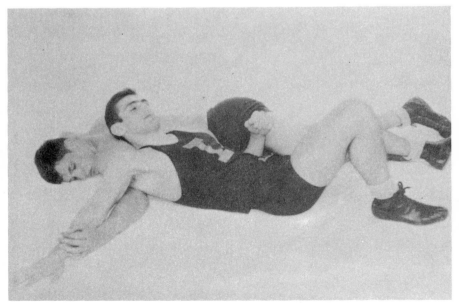

66C Arch back on the opponent's shoulder and arm as a means of immobilizing him.

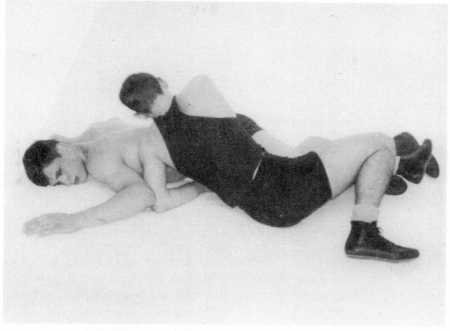

66D Turn in to a position of advantage on top.

6

Conditioning

ORIENTATION TO WORKOUTS

Wrestling demands rigid conditioning. A program of strenuous exercise, sensible diet, good health habits, and regular sleep is essential.

The Patterson System requires the wrestler to run a mile to warm up prior to engaging in any actual wrestling. The mile run raises the body temperature and thereby decreases the chances of sustaining an injury.

The pace of the first 3/4 of the mile is a slow jog. The jogging is done forward, backward, and sideward. The last quarter of a mile is done by alternating 100 yard sprints with 110 yard jogs.

PREWORKOUT EXERCISES

After the mile run, the wrestler is expected to hang from an overhead chinning bar for one minute. This is followed by bridging exercises. Bridging strengthens the neck muscles. These muscles are exercised by rolling the head back and forth, and from side to side. The neck while supporting the weight of the body also acts as a pivot to enable the wrestler to turn over from his back to his stomach.

A variation of this bridging exercise is done from standing. Help is generally needed with this variation until balance is learned. After acquiring the strength and flexibility necessary to lean back and touch the mat, assistance is no longer required.

Three sets of push ups follow these bridging exercises. The first set is done without weight. The second set is done with a teammate sitting on the wrestler's back offering just enough resistance so that no more than ten push ups can be done. The second set is then repeated a third time.

Push ups are an excellent exercise because they are quite similar to the movement required to get from a prone position on the mat to the hands and knees.

A second kind of push up, done from a handstand position, can be substituted for the type described above. It is first learned from a handstand position while having the feet propped against a wall or held by a teammate.

To be certain that all the major muscles of the body are exercised sit ups are also included. These are done with or without weights, on level ground or an inclined board. They may also be done while bending over the edge of a table or bench.

Finally the wrestler is required to climb a twenty-foot rope three times. This builds a powerful grip and upper body strength. In the absence of a rope, pegboard climbing can be substituted.

The wrestler then goes to the wrestling room and is given a review and/or instruction on new holds. Afterward he practices these holds for thirty minutes or more before wrestling a four-, six-, or eight-minute match (depending upon the time of the year). He holds for a few minutes, before wrestling again. After wrestling the second bout, he cools down and rests before wrestling a third time. Each of these matches is against a different opponent or against two wrestlers alternating as one opponent.

The best conditioning for wrestling is to wrestle, and wrestle hard. Endurance for wrestling is built by wrestling.

The last ten or fifteen minutes of the workout are spent on practicing holds and set ups. Following this the wrestler cools down by hanging from a horizontal bar for a full minute. This decreases the likelihood of his breaking a sweat and catching a cold after showering and leaving the gym.

HAND STAND PUSH UP #1

67A This exercise develops the arms and shoulders. It requires the wrestler to press his own weight. The wrestler is assisted in maintaining an erect position by having a partner grasp him around the knees. The wrestler's entire weight is supported on his hands. He bends his arms until his nose touches the mat and then he returns to the original position.

HAND STAND PUSH UP #2

68A The wrestler begins by facing his partner and kicking up to a handstand. The partner spots him. In the handstand position his feet should be spread to complement the partner's efforts to assist him.

68B The exercise begins with the wrestler's arms being fully extended. The partner holds his legs at the ankles so he will not fall as he lowers and raises himself from the mat. To increase the resistance one arm can be used while the other is kept folded behind the back. Balancing, however, often becomes difficult.

REVERSE PUSH UP

69A This exercise is designed to develop the muscles of the back of the upper arms and the shoulder area. To perform the exercise the wrestler places his hands on the mat under his shoulders and pushes up into a high arch. His head should be kept back so he is looking down at the surface of the mat.

EXTENSION PUSH UP

70A This exercise is designed to strengthen the arms, shoulders, fore-arms, wrists, and grip. With his body held rigid in an extended front support position, the wrestler lowers himself to the mat until his chest almost touches. He then pushes back up to the original starting position. During this exercise, he should keep his back straight and the weight of his body over his finger tips.

WRESTLER'S BRIDGE

71A Bridging is an exercise that develops the muscles of the back, legs, and neck. The wrestler should arch so that the weight of his body is supported only by the back of his head and the soles of his feet. His hands should be slightly greater than shoulder's width apart with the fingers pointing forward.

The exercise is performed by rocking back and forth on his head so his nose and chin touch the mat. This will strengthen the muscles used for bridging out of pinning holds. The resistance can be increased by having a partner sit on his chest during the exercise.

ASSISTED BACK ARCH #1

72A This exercise is designed to develop and condition the muscles of the back, neck, and legs. The wrestler grasps his partner's hand and bends backward until his hands touch the mat. He then raises and lowers himself with as little assistance as possible. He should attempt to place his hands as close to his feet as possible.

ASSISTED BACK ARCH #2

73A This exercise is designed to develop flexibility in the spinal column and to condition the muscles of the legs, arms, and especially the back. A partner is used to help the wrestler overcome the uncertainty of falling back.

73B The wrestler flexes his legs and thighs, and extends back until his hands are resting on the mat. The partner offers assistance by placing a hand at the center of his back for support. The exercise should be done slowly, especially at the beginning.

PROGRAM OF WEIGHT CONTROL

No conditioning program is complete without a properly controlled diet. The Patterson System employs the following reducing diet. This diet was specifically designed for wrestlers by Professor Floyd Boyds, M.D., University of Illinois, Urbana.

Breakfast: 1 small glass (4 oz.) of unsweetened fruit juice.
1 medium serving (½ cup) of any HOT cereal with skimmed milk, and sweetened (if desired) with 1 tablespoon of honey. (OR: 1 poached or boiled egg and 2 strips of bacon).
1 slice of dark, whole-grain bread or toast with ½ pat butter.
Coffee or tea as desired (cream and sugar omitted).

Lunch: 1 small glass (4 oz.) of unsweetened vegetable juice.
           1 serving *each* of any two vegetables listed.
           1 medium serving of lean meat, fish, or cheese.
           1 ordinary glass of skimmed milk.
           1 slice of dark, whole-grain bread or toast with ½ pat
           butter.
           For dessert, 1 serving of any fruit listed.
           Coffee or tea as desired (cream and sugar omitted).
Dinner: (OPTIONAL) 1 cup of any clear soup—fat removed.
           1 serving *each* of any two vegetables listed.
           1 medium serving of lean meat, fish, or cheese.
           1 ordinary glass of skimmed milk.
           1 slice of dark, whole-grain bread or toast with ½ pat
           butter.
           For dessert (if desired), 1 serving of any fruit listed.
           (OR: 1 serving of any selected dessert listed).
           Coffee or tea as desired (cream and sugar omitted).

Classification of Vegetables and Fruits:

5% Vegetables (1 serving—1 cup)		*10% Vegetables* (1 serving—½ cup)	
Asparagus	Broccoli	Carrots	Turnips
Brussel Sprouts	Sauerkraut	Radishes	Rutabagas
Celery	String Beans	Onions	Pumpkin
Cauliflower	Spinach	Mushrooms	Beets
Cabbage	Lettuce	Green Olives	Artichokes
Kale	Ripe Olives	Green Beans	Squash
Chard	Watercress	Avocados	Peas
Tomatoes	Rhubarb		

5% Fruits (1 serving—1 cup)		*10% Fruits* (1 serving—½ cup)	
Blackberries	Cantaloupe	Apricots	Peaches
Grapefruit	Strawberries	Raspberries	Pineapple
Gooseberries		Watermelon	(fresh)
		Oranges	Lemons

Selected Desserts

½ cup of baked custard	½ cup of junket
½ cup of ice or sherbet	½ cup of jello

Weight should be lost gradually on a well-balanced diet. As a means of evaluating whether a wrestler should be reducing, the "Pinch Test" devised by retired Oklahoma State University wrestling coach Art Griffith is used. The test is a safe and reliable method of determining whether a wrestler is carrying too much fat.

If the pinched skin fold around the middle of the stomach is the same thickness as the pinched skin on the forehead, the wrestler is considered to be at his optimum minimal weight. However, if the thickness at the waistline is more than that of the forehead, the wrestler is carrying excess weight.

Obviously, there are more sophisticated methods of determining a wrestler's best weight, but none are quite as simple.

Bibliography

Carson, Ray F. "Criteria for the Selection of Escape and Reversal Techniques." *Scholastic Coach* (January 1970), pp. 69–70.

———. "The Short Sit-Out A Dangerous Wrestling Technique." *Scholastic Wrestling News* (February 15, 1970), p. 7.

———. "Standing Versus on the Mat Escapes and Reversals." *Scholastic Coach* (May 1970), pp. 16–18.

———. *Systematic Championship Wrestling.* South Brunswick, New Jersey: A. S. Barnes and Company, Inc., 1973.

———. "Twisting Arm Fireman's Carry." *Scholastic Coach* (May 1971), pp. 56+.

———. "Stand Up and Wrestle." *Scholastic Coach* (September 1972), pp. 44+.

———. *"A Critical Analysis of Escape and Reversal Techniques Employed in N.C.A.A. Championship Wrestling Matches from 1952 to 1955 and from 1956 to 1969."* Director's thesis, School of Health, Physical Education, and Recreation, Indiana University, Bloomington, Indiana, 1969.

Gallagher, Edward C., and Peery, Rex. *Wrestling.* New York: Ronald Press, 1951.

Griffith, Art. "A New Style of Amateur Wrestling." *Athletic Journal* (December 1946), pp. 22+.

———. "Maturity and Experience is the Answer." *Mentor* (March 1954), pp. 26+.

———. "The Scissors Hold in Wrestling." *Athletic Journal* (February 1937), pp. 20+.

———. "Wrestling for Mavericks." *Athletic Journal* (February 1950), pp. 26+.

Keen, Clifford. "Edward Clark Gallagher." *Mentor* (April 1954), pp. 24+.

————, Speidel, Charles M., and Swartz, Raymond H. *Championship Wrestling*. United States Naval Institute. Menasha, Wisconsin: George Banta Company, Inc., 1961.

Nelson, Dale O. "Improving Performance by Utilizing Fundamental Principles of Movement." *Athletic Journal* (November 1958), pp. 26+.

Patterson, Buel R. in "Coaches' Clinic." *Athletic Journal* (December 1967), p. 6.

————, and Carson, Ray F. *Principles of Championship Wrestling*. South Brunswick, New Jersey: A. S. Barnes and Company, Inc., 1972.

————, and Carson, Ray F. "Wrestling." *Encyclopedia of Physical Education*. Edited by Thomas K. Cureton, Jr. Washington, D. C.: The American Association for Health, Physical Education, and Recreation, 1974.

Turner, William. *A Cinematiographical Analysis of a Wrestling Technique—Control of Opponent From Behind*. Master's thesis, Department of Physical Education, University of Illinois, Champaign, Illinois, 1959.

Wilson, Charles M. *The Magnificent Scufflers*. Brattleboro, Vermont: Stephen Greene Press, 1959.

Yuhasz, Mike, Leyshon, Glynn, and Salter, Bill. *Basic Wrestling*. Ontario, Canada: University of Western Ontario Press, 1963.

Index